Comments on other *Amazing Stories* from readers & reviewers

*"Tightly written volumes filled with lots of wit and humour
about famous and infamous Canadians."*
Eric Shackleton, *The Globe and Mail*

*"The heightened sense of drama and intrigue, combined with a
good dose of human interest is what sets* Amazing Stories *apart."*
Pamela Klaffke, *Calgary Herald*

*"This is popular history as it should be... For this price,
buy two and give one to a friend."*
Terry Cook, a reader from Ottawa, on **Rebel Women**

*"Glasner creates the moment of the explosion itself in
graphic detail...she builds detail upon gruesome detail
to create a convincingly authentic picture."*
Peggy McKinnon, *The Sunday Herald,* on **The Halifax Explosion**

*"It was wonderful...I found I could not put it down.
I was sorry when it was completed."*
Dorothy F. from Manitoba on **Marie-Anne Lagimodière**

*"Stories are rich in description, and bristle
with a clever, stylish realness."*
Mark Weber, *Central Alberta Advisor,* on **Ghost Town Stories II**

*"A compelling read. Bertin...has selected only the most intriguing
tales, which she narrates with a wealth of detail."*
Joyce Glasner, *New Brunswick Reader,* on **Strange Events**

*"The resulting book is one readers will want to share
with all the women in their lives."*
Lynn Martel, *Rocky Mountain Outlook,* on **Women Explorers**

LEGENDARY NHL COACHES

AMAZING STORIES®

LEGENDARY NHL COACHES

Stars of Hockey's Golden Age

HOCKEY

by Glenn Wilkins

PUBLISHED BY ALTITUDE PUBLISHING CANADA LTD.
1500 Railway Avenue, Canmore, Alberta T1W 1P6
www.altitudepublishing.com
www.amazingstories.ca
1-800-957-6888

Extreme care has been taken to ensure that all information presented in
this book is accurate and up to date. Neither the author nor the
publisher can be held responsible for any errors.

Publisher	Stephen Hutchings
Associate Publisher	Kara Turner
Editors	Linda Aspen-Baxter and Nancy Mackenzie
Cover and Layout	Bryan Pezzi

We acknowledge the financial support of the Government
of Canada through the Book Publishing Industry Development
Program (BPIDP) for our publishing activities.

Altitude GreenTree Program
Altitude Publishing will plant twice as many trees as were used
in the manufacturing of this product.

National Library of Canada Cataloguing in Publication Data

Wilkins, Glenn, 1956-
    Legendary NHL coaches / Glenn Wilkins.

(Amazing stories)
Includes bibliographical references.
ISBN 1-55439-101-6

    1. Hockey coaches--Biography. 2. National Hockey League--
Biography. I. Title. II. Series: Amazing stories (Canmore, Alta.)

GV848.5.A1W56 2006   796.962'092'2   C2005-906887-6

Amazing Stories® is a registered trademark of Altitude Publishing Canada Ltd.

Printed and bound in Canada by Friesens
2 4 6 8 9 7 5 3 1

For Marian, my wife, who often functions as *my* coach. No fan of pro sports (many times she's jokingly reminded me that our cable service doesn't pick up TSN), she has nonetheless proven over the years that she is a big fan of mine.

Her love and support through this project has been vital.

Contents

Prologue

George "Punch" Imlach's Toronto Maple Leafs fashioned an ending to their playoff run Robert Ripley wouldn't believe.

Less than a minute from an improbable victory against a favoured Montreal team, there they were holding the Canadiens off with a selection of superannuated veterans who would find their way to immortality — Stanley, Horton, Pulford, Kelly, and Armstrong. Behind them in the goal crease, the doomed hero, Terry Sawchuk, had withstood the best efforts the Hab snipers could muster.

The Canadien cage was empty, and the Leafs were leading 2–1. Like the proud, battle-scarred veteran he fancied himself to be, Imlach went into this final minute with the foot soldiers who had gotten him to victory in the past ... despite the young blood on his bench. He sent 41 year old defenceman, Allan Stanley — not the best face-off man in the world — up against Jean Beliveau.

Forward Bob Pulford had tangled with Imlach a number of times. However, when he recalled the story, he saw symbolism in his coach's selection of George Armstrong, Tim Horton, Red Kelly, Allan Stanley, and himself. All who watched knew it would be a swan song for those five men and the end of their dynasty.

Stanley swiped at the dropped puck and barreled into Beliveau as Kelly slipped it to a striding Pulford. He passed to captain Armstrong, who sent the puck into the open Montreal net for the insurance marker. The seconds ticked down on the new digital clock at the old Gardens, which was about to go Stanley Cup nuts for the last time. Montreal may have had the World's Fair, but the Toronto Maple Leafs had won a centennial year Stanley Cup. Punch had gone with his gut and come up a winner… for the last time.

Introduction

The role of the coach in hockey is a misunderstood, and often, thankless one. During stoppages in play on a hockey telecast, fans are used to shots of the coach looking haggard and harried, pacing behind the bench, wondering and worrying what will come next in the game. However, what's probably going on behind the eyes would present a different image: one of a sponge, taking in fully all the good and bad points of the team's performance. Either in the dressing room between periods or at practice between games, the coach communicates to the players about adjustments he deems necessary.

There is so little a coach can do while a hockey game is actually in progress apart from shout encouragement to the troops and make sure the line changes are executed cleanly. Hockey is one of only two sports like this; soccer is the other. A football coach can send in a play to the quarterback, after making adjustments to what the defence has thrown at his team. Basketball coaches can call time out with maddening regularity, either to discuss defensive setup or reverse the unfavourable momentum. Baseball managers can call individual pitches. However, a sport that requires flow leaves the coach little time to breathe, let alone make adjustments. Rather, it's a case of turning control of the game over to the players, allowing them room to react and to find the time to correct what's wrong. The good coaches already know that; the great ones knew it long ago.

These pages feature seven such men, coaches who fashioned dynasties throughout the building years of the National Hockey League. They kept men of muscle and sweat under control and playing to the very best of their potential. These coaches had to play other roles, those of mentor, cheerleader, father figure, jailer, paymaster ... but most of all, boss.

As the game's demographics, pay structure, and fan base have changed, so, too, has the coach's role. Today the coach has to allow for more constant player travel, a more sophisticated level of expectation from fans and media, a more dynamic level of strategy against other teams, and more labour developments, including salary caps.

There is little wonder that the coach's lot is often not a happy one.

The coaches featured here, were, in their day, representative of the game's gold standard. Their personalities, attractive and otherwise, continue to merit our attention to this day.

Chapter 1
Lester Patrick:
The Innovator

f Scotty Bowman and Toe Blake were hockey's version of Generals Patton and Montgomery, Lester Patrick would have to be considered its Thomas Edison or Leonardo da Vinci. Aside from his record as player, coach, and general manager, Patrick was responsible for a variety of innovations still in use in hockey today, including the playoff format.

Patrick achieved success in the spring of 1928 when his New York Rangers reached the Stanley Cup finals in only their second year of operation. History shows Patrick had more invested in the club — physically, emotionally, and financially — during that Cup run than most coaches or managers do during playoffs.

The Rangers had been brought together from rinks all over

North America. To rise that far that fast provided a heady time for a bunch of young men experiencing hockey glory for the first time. Soon events seemed to bear out the poet T. S. Eliot's dictum that April is the cruelest month. For starters, a scheduling clash gave the circus first dibs on Madison Square Garden. This forced the Rangers to try and win their first Cup entirely on the road. All games in the best-of-five series were played at the venerable Montreal Forum, and goalie Clint Benedict stood 10 feet tall in a 2–0 Maroon victory in game one.

A pivotal moment came in the first period of game two. It was April 7, 1928. The deadly Maroon sniper, Nels Stewart — Old Poison himself, who would amass 324 goals in his career — got off a laser beam that caught Ranger net minder, Lorne Chabot, under the left eye. Down went Lorne, out like a light, blood running down his cheek. The Ranger players on the ice and on the bench, not to mention their manager, were stunned. This was the era before the slapshot, but it also predated common use of the face mask and clubs with a spare goalie in the trunk. As a result, there was no understudy ready to jump in at a moment's notice. It was the stiffest test to which the New York Rangers had been put in their young history.

Their keeper was done for the night, and maybe the series. Once that reality had set in, Lester Patrick scurried about in search of a replacement. A quick mental scan helped him recall that future Hall of Fame goalie Alex Connell, of the Ottawa Senators, was in the gallery that night. The problem would be solved, if only the Maroons would give the okay.

One can only imagine the reaction in the Montreal locker room when Patrick made his pitch to the Maroons. After all, why would they give the enemy a loaded Magnum to shoot them with?

Patrick returned to his team's dressing room and broke the news that they wouldn't be playing in front of Connell. The Rangers were behind in a short series, in hostile territory, facing some of the most feared sharpshooters in the game, without a goalie, and running out of options.

Opinion is divided on who suggested Patrick go into the net himself. Maybe it was centre Frank Boucher, maybe someone from the front office, or maybe Patrick himself. As seconds ticked by and folks were anxious to get on with the game, Patrick appeared more and more the obvious choice, doddering old man or not.

Patrick would be playing an unfamiliar position. He had never donned the heavy pads Chabot had to carry night after night in the Stanley Cup finals against a team serving notice it was taking no prisoners. Nothing Patrick had encountered in his playing days had prepared him for this!

After what seemed an eternal intermission, the shock of silver hair atop the head that led the Rangers back onto the ice was equaled by the shock in the Forum stalls. Yes, this was Lester Patrick, the man who ran the practices and signed the cheques twice a month, skating into the net against the mighty Maroons. The buzz in the crowd seemed to say that the remainder of the game was going to be a cakewalk.

Not at all, for the Rangers still had Ching Johnson and Taffy Abel, stay-at-home defencemen extraordinaire, who made sure nobody got near their boss. Finally, early in the third, Ranger winger Bill Cook split the Maroon defence to beat Benedict with the game's first goal. At the other end, there was Lester Patrick, quieting the murmurs and stopping shot after shot. He made the one-goal lead stand up until 14 minutes after Cook's marker, when Nels Stewart, whose earlier drive had flattened Chabot, deked Lester out of position and slipped one home.

With the score tied, the pressure was truly on. How long could Lester Patrick, coach, manager, entrepreneur, builder, showman ... *and goalie*, hold on to prevent his team from falling behind two games against the marauding Maroons? As regulation ended with the 1–1 tie, he had to last into overtime. Fortunately, the agony of Patrick and the Rangers was short-lived. Boucher seized the game after seven minutes of the extra frame and found enough open twine to beat Benedict for the game-winner.

Lester was a tall, gangly-looking figure, but when mobbed by his teammates/employees after the winning goal, he must have appeared twice that tall. This was more than the story of a mogul removing his tie and rolling up his sleeves to protect his investment, à la Mario Lemieux or Michael Jordan. It was probably the first case of a legend returning from the hockey sidelines to step in for his team and shine when it needed him the most. Call-up Joe Miller suited up for the next three

Lester Patrick

games and proved just as stingy. He notched a shutout in game four and a 2–1 victory in the fifth and clinching contest to give the New York Rangers their first Stanley Cup triumph. Patrick, however, was the real story.

Lester Patrick was born in Drummondville, Quebec, in December 1883. He was the eldest son of a successful lumberman who eventually took his fortune with him out west and settled the family in Nelson, British Columbia. Lester's brother, Frank, was born two years later.

Patrick was a young player in the era when teams had seven men on the ice. The seventh, called the rover, was able to roam the ice and not be restricted to laying back in wait for the other team's rush. One of the first men to see his name engraved on the Stanley Cup as both player and coach, Patrick first carved out his niche with the Montreal Wanderers. He scored the game winning and insurance goals in 1906 to break the backs and end the three-year Cup streak of the fabled Ottawa Silver Seven. Patrick stayed with the Wanderers for another year, while brother Frank completed his studies at McGill University, before joining father Joe in Nelson. It was there that the family made its next big impression on the greatest game in the world.

British Columbia winters are known more for their unpredictability than for their hardiness, which extends to their ice surfaces. The solution was to manufacture ice so that it could be skated on all year round. Manufactured ice was used in Lester and Frank's small rink in Nelson. The team occupying that rink won the BC title. Lester Patrick was a key player on that club, before he found himself in the middle of a bidding war for his services between professional teams in Renfrew and Ottawa.

Patrick wasn't wild about the idea of going to Renfrew, which he thought was just a dot on the map. Initially, he demanded $1,500 a season from the team in the nation's capital and $3,000 from Renfrew, reckoning that no one would part with that kind of cash. (The average annual wage in many Canadian industries at that time was about $400.) To his surprise, Renfrew wired back and ordered him to report at once — *for the three grand he wanted!* Lester replied he'd pack up and head east if the team would offer Frank $2,000 — *terms to which Renfrew also agreed!* Owner M.J. O'Brien was putting his money where his mouth was. He wanted to show the hockey world he was serious about winning the Stanley Cup by bringing in not only the Patricks, but also the legendary Fred "Cyclone" Taylor. Even so, with all this loot floating around, the Millionaires came up a few dollars short of Cup glory.

When Joe Patrick sold his business in 1911, the brothers returned West and launched a professional loop of their own. They put up rinks in Victoria and Vancouver — the latter's capacity a staggering 10,000 seats — and lured away stars like Fred "Cyclone" Taylor, Moose Johnson, Newsy Lalonde, and goaltender Bert Lindsay. The new Pacific Coast Hockey Association grew in time to include teams in Alberta, Saskatchewan, and the state of Washington. Its credibility got a mammoth shot in the arm when Frank's Vancouver Millionaires won the Stanley Cup in 1915, followed by the Seattle Metropolitans in 1917 and Lester's Victoria Cougars in 1925.

All the while, the brothers needed a new rack for all the hats they were wearing — building the rinks and promoting the teams to fill the stands; hiring the players and signing their cheques; running the league and making out the schedules; drafting rule changes; coaching ... and, yes, playing! The forward pass and the rushing defenceman; allowing goaltenders to fall to the ice to smother a shot; boarding penalties, delayed penalties, and the penalty shot; assists on goals; substitution on the fly; blue lines dividing the rink into three zones; numbers on uniforms; and ultimately, the playoff format — all were the handiwork of either Frank or Lester Patrick.

Lester Patrick was a restless soul, always thinking, promoting, experimenting, and trying new things. In the spring of 1908, the Patricks, accompanied by Cyclone Taylor and a galaxy of other great stars, were in Manhattan to play exhibition games at the old St. Nicholas Arena and to take in the sights of the great metropolis.

Taylor told his biographer 70 years later, "They got a lot more out of New York than just another hockey experience. In their off hours, they saw all they could of the city, and we saw little of them. They always gave the impression that they were filing information away for future reference."

Years later, Tommy Gorman, who ran the New York Americans, recalled, "Lester didn't adjust to New York. New York adjusted to him."

The bubble burst on the boys' Pacific Coast Hockey League in the mid-1920s. American magnates were outbidding the Patricks for new talent, much as Lester and Frank had done 15 years before. It seemed natural that Lester

Patrick and the city of New York would hook up once again, thereafter becoming an inseparable pair.

The former Hamilton Tigers started the charge to New York as the Americans in 1925, and their success convinced hockey operators that the game could thrive and flourish in the city that never sleeps. Could the citizens of the great metropolis accommodate two collections of hockey players, even if those puck chasers mostly hailed from far-flung Canadian outposts? George "Tex" Rickard, president of Madison Square Garden, decided to give it a go. In honour of Rickard, sportswriters nicknamed the team "Tex's Rangers." Somehow the name stuck, as did the diagonal positioning of the letters down the front of their blue uniforms.

After the team had a home and all the cosmetic changes were in place, Lester Patrick got the call from Tex and his men to corral the Rangers and guide them on their Stanley Cup trail. Factually, Lester Patrick was not the father of the New York Rangers, at least not the biological one. It might be said the waif was left on Patrick's stoop with the sacking of Conn Smythe.

Smythe, the University of Toronto-educated firebrand, had travelled hither and yon throughout North America in the summer of 1926 to assemble the nucleus of the team that would proudly don the NY blue. Obviously, Smythe knew where to look; by panning in scattered ponds, Conn found hockey gold. There was the towering defenceman from the Michigan Sault named Clarence Abel; Winnipegger Ivan "Ching" Johnson, a former cook on the CPR; a pair of Cooks named Bill and Fred who would patrol the wings for years to come; and complementing them all, a slick centre named Frank Boucher, who would go on to coach the Rangers during the war years and wear the general manager's cap after that.

But New York … New York was a helluva town, even then. The bellow of the Roaring 20s issued loudest from the isle of joy, even in an era of speakeasies. The Yanks still ruled the baseball roost, with Babe Ruth and Lou Gehrig smacking home runs out of the Bronx. John McGraw and his National League Giants held court at Manhattan's Polo Grounds. Boxing was the big thing at Madison Square Garden, with the likes of Jack Dempsey, Gene Tunney, Harry Greb, and Mickey Walker shining brightest. There were six-day bike races, vaudeville houses, Coney Island during the summer, and apart from motion pictures finding their voice, there were Carnegie Hall and 63 legitimate theatres on Broadway! Competition for the entertainment dollar was fierce.

Given this situation, someone in the front office at Madison Square Garden decided that Conn Smythe was not showy enough to sell the game in a market like New York. Before the puck dropped in the Rangers' first game, Conn Smythe was bounced in favour of Lester Patrick. He cultivated hard-boiled Manhattan sportswriters and educated them on the beauty of what legendary sportswriter Damon Runyon (whose stories are used in *Guys and Dolls*) called "a game I do not fail to misunderstand."

Lester Patrick: The Innovator

On that auspicious 1926 opening night against the defending Stanley Cup champion Montreal Maroons, Lester Patrick, aged 43 and already a legend, was at the wheel of an "expansion" team. This is a term that in today's world of 30-team leagues would connote "pushover," a rag-tag collection of has-beens, no-goods, and never-will-bes. Indeed, Rickard himself pointedly asked Smythe, just one of many Garden spectators that night, whether the Broadway Blueshirts could "hold" the Maroons to less than 10 goals.

Conn, not batting an eye, replied, "Hold 'em, nothing. You'll beat 'em."

His erstwhile charges proved him right, making a lone Bill Cook goal stand up for a 1–0 victory. The team continued to play well all year long, taking first place in the NHL's American Division by 11 points over Boston, before bowing in the first round of the playoffs to those same Bruins. The orphan may have been left for Patrick to raise, but he had more than learned to walk! A year later, the kid was raising the Stanley Cup high over his head.

Besides his many jobs as a hockey operator, Patrick exhibited many different personalities. Boucher would say his former boss was by turns arrogant and short-tempered, pleasant and excitable, kind and sarcastic, pompous and gentle, depending on the circumstances. It has also been said that he could carry a grudge for years.

Commentator Dick Irvin recalled how his father, then piloting the Leafs, got into a heated argument with Patrick behind the benches in the late 1930s during a game at Maple Leaf Gardens. The two went nose-to-nose, coming within an ace of taking swings at each other. The feelings remained so hard that after he returned to New York, Patrick surveyed the hockey pictures on the walls of Madison Square Garden and took down the ones of Dick Irvin. Time eventually healed all wounds, and the two hardheads resolved their differences in the stands of a ballgame in Montreal nearly 20 years later. When Dick Sr. died in 1957, one of the first telegrams of condolence Dick Irvin's mother received was from Lester Patrick, suggesting inspirational Bible passages.

Hockey historian Brian McFarlane quoted Alex Shibicky, a player from those great Ranger teams of the 1930s, who recalled a man of a "high moral code. He had a tremendous amount of personal feeling toward his players. He was an educated man in a tough sport. He would conduct classes in the Ranger dressing room, asking the capital city of nations and the names of rivers." He wished to build his players up as human beings, and not just as hockey players.

McFarlane also quoted Babe Pratt, a defenceman from his 1940 team, as saying, "You just couldn't be around Lester for long without learning something." Reporters who hung around the Ranger dressing room found that out in frequent, informal information sessions about the game. These rink tutorials enlightened many of the younger scribes, but they flummoxed the legendary Damon Runyon, a sportswriter who was very knowledgeable about baseball and boxing.

Damon was baffled by the game of hockey, despite everything Patrick tried to do to educate him.

Indeed, folks discussing Patrick remember a teetotaler who watched his pennies. Nothing chemical would slow him down in achieving his ambitions for himself or his team. Patrick may not have been any more of a tightwad than fellow NHL general managers, but even his own flesh-and-blood knew that dickering with Patrick for a raise elicited more than a few squeaks. Lynn Patrick was the top scorer among NHL left wingers one year, making the first all-star team. When he brought those points up in contract negotiations the following fall, Patrick told his progeny and star, "Yeah, but I made sure you had good linemates." Lynn Patrick, all-star and feared sniper, had to sign for what his boss/father was offering — the same salary as the year before.

Patrick's efforts at selling the Rangers did not extend to bending the truth. There was one public relations man who tried renaming Oliver Reinikka, of Finnish extract, "Ollie Rocco" to appeal to Italian fans, and Chabot to "Chabotsky" to attract Jewish customers. The publicist even went so far as to suggest in the papers that Bill Cook would be "kidnapped," but then "returned" in time for the next game. Thankfully, this two-bit shill was soon shown the door. Hockey in New York would have to stand or fall on its own merits, for that was Lester Patrick's way.

To Lester Patrick, hockey was a game of movement. He wanted his players in motion at all times and to have the puck carrier hit a teammate with a pass on the fly. He knew this would provide better flow to the game, and did Patrick have the skaters to keep that flow going! Bill Cook led the league in scoring twice and compiled 229 career goals. Brother Bun didn't light the lamp as much, but he did drive defenders crazy with his skating style. Frank Boucher carried the puck as if "on a string," as Foster Hewitt once said. There was a fair complement of toughness on the Rangers squad, as evidenced by Abel, Johnson, and Murray Murdoch, the "iron man" of hockey, who played for 600 straight games.

The Patricks first showed the signs of a family dynasty in New York. It was one that would extend to the present day, with sons and grandsons also making their mark on the game, not just travelling on the coattails of their famous father and/or uncle.

Bringing Lynn and younger son Murray (Muzz) onto the roster was something Lester Patrick held out against. He feared charges of favouritism, until the manager of another club spotted Lynn on the Montreal Royals senior league squad. He told Lester, "Either put him on your list, or I'll put him on ours."

Muzz joined the big club three years later in 1937. He didn't enjoy the Hall of Fame career that his father, uncle, and brother did, but he proved rock steady on the Ranger blue line for four years, including 1940. This was the last Stanley Cup celebration the Patrick family and fans of Ranger blue knew for more than half a century. After all, as the old saw goes, offence sells tickets, but defence wins championships.

Lester Patrick coached the Rangers for 13 years. He missed the playoffs only once and added another Cup over Smythe's Leafs in 1933, before turning the reins over to Frank Boucher and concentrating solely on his general manager's duties. He retired as GM in 1946, again in favour of Boucher, and he carried on in something of an advisory role. Relations broke down between the two men over Boucher's reluctance to act on his advice, a breach that time did not heal. Lester died in June 1960; his brother Frank died four weeks later.

The royal Patrick line continues to the present day. Lynn continued after his playing days as coach of the Bruins in the 1950s and eventually became general manager. He then became the first general manager of the expansion St. Louis Blues in 1967, bringing Scotty Bowman on as his head coach. Muzz had a brief spell as a minor league coach. Lynn's son, Craig, was assistant coach and assistant GM with the "Miracle on Ice" US Olympic team that struck gold at Lake Placid in 1980. Then he assumed the GM's role with a Pittsburgh Penguin team that hoisted two straight Stanley Cups in the 1990s. Brother Glenn played briefly in the NHL with St. Louis, Oakland, and Cleveland, and in the WHA with Edmonton. Muzz's son Dick is now president and part owner of the Washington Capitals. It seems everywhere you look in hockey, you see a Patrick!

As for the co-founder of that dynasty, Lester Patrick left

his mark on the game as player, innovator, showman, coach, and teacher. When asked for his views on coaching hockey, his reply was simple. "I look for the leaders, and let them lead. I give my last instructions in the dressing room just before the game; then I sit and let them think about whatever they like. Then I look at Bill Cook, one of my stars, who has already made his mark. Is he at ease? Not on your life. He's a bundle of nerves, just aching for the game to start to break the tension. I need the Bill Cooks (who I can count on) for the inspired kind of hockey needed to win championships. The other players, when it comes right down to the crunch, will follow the Bill Cooks. Then I just tag along, and enjoy it."

Certainly, Lester Patrick gave hockey fans down through the ages much to enjoy, and the game recognizes his achievements. For the longest time, the NHL had a Patrick Division. Starting in 1966, the Rangers awarded the Lester Patrick Trophy, which is given annually to the person contributing most to the game of hockey in the United States. Past winners have included Frank Boucher, Murray Murdoch, Gordie Howe, Bobby Hull, Wayne Gretzky, Scotty Bowman ... and Lynn and Craig Patrick. Lester would be pleased!

The image of a man thought past his prime, whose hair had turned white, gliding into the net in a relief role and stopping 18 of 19 shots in a Stanley Cup final game, will linger in the memory of hockey fans for ages to come. He gave his team a chance to win when it needed him the most.

Chapter 2
Art Ross:
The Eccentric

Game one of the 1939 Stanley Cup finals was a toss-up. The fact that it was going into overtime left Boston coach Art Ross in a quandary. Dave Kerr, the goalie for the opposing New York Rangers, had stopped every shot but one in 60 minutes, and the Bruins had prided themselves on their scoring touch.

Then Ross looked down the end of the Bruin bench and saw a 5 foot 9 inch, 160-pound slip of a player by the name of Mel Hill. Ironically enough, the product of Glenboro, Manitoba had been a reject from the Ranger camp only a couple of years before. Because of his size and age (at the time, Hill was only a teenager), Hill expected to be dumped by Lester Patrick's team. However, soon after, he was picked up by Ross' Boston Bruins. In the most important series of his life, Mel Hill was to be given the chance to come to life.

Hill had scored only 10 goals during the regular season, but Ross had a plan. Just before the puck was dropped for the extra frame, Ross notified his all-star centre, Bill Cowley, to start feeding passes to the youngster Hill. "They're watching Roy Conacher (the other winger) so carefully, it would be better to pass to Hill."

It took three overtimes, but Cowley got Hill in the clear and slid him a pass, which Mel deposited into the cage behind Kerr. Hill did it again in game two — in the first overtime — when he converted a Cowley with a 40-foot blast that found the back of the net. Boston took a 2–0 lead in the best-of-seven final. Hill was quiet until game seven, when the contest was into its third extra frame. Again, Cowley saw Hill streaking in on the defence. He put the pass right on the tape of Hill's stick, and Hill lifted the puck over Kerr to give the Bruins the Stanley Cup. His insertion into the line-up, presumably at the last minute, made coach Art Ross look like a genius.

Even though Art Ross was a defenceman in playing days, his offensive output as a player totaled 85 goals in 167 regular season games. Art Ross held such a commanding position as player, coach, general manager, promoter, and innovator, that he has a trophy named after him in the NHL, awarded each year to the player who leads the league in points (goals and assists added together). To Art Ross, hockey owes the way nets and pucks are designed, as well as the strategy of pulling a goaltender for an extra attacker late in tight games.

Boston fans of three generations recognize that their club may not have survived if it weren't for a showman like Art Ross, who always created an angle to draw fans to the Garden. This was a team that needed all the help it could get. The fact that one family had deep enough pockets to bankroll it along with two other teams or shut them down with the snap of two fingers sometimes created obstacles to Ross's ability to acquire the best players.

As coach, Art Ross was a man of few words, which was not necessarily good news. Any Boston Bruin player who screwed up could count on his boss coming into the dressing room at intermission, lighting up a smoke, Bogie-style, then circling the room in search of the offender, glaring at him with what players called his "bad eye," pointing at the unfortunate's head, and barking the words, "Use it." Point made.

Like many rival coaches in the NHL, Art Ross drew a general manager's salary as well and negotiated player contracts with a clenched fist. A young Milt Schmidt recalled asking Ross for a $500 raise in 1936, only to be told that the GM would have to leave the room and bounce it off Bruin owner, Charles Adams. When Ross returned a few minutes later, he relayed to his 18 year old centre that Mr. Adams didn't go along with it. Schmidt dutifully signed, then headed over to Adams' office to inquire why the money was not in the budget. Outside the office, Adams' secretary indicated that her boss hadn't arrived yet and wouldn't be in for the rest of the week! Years later, Schmidt recalled that first impression of Art Ross with a laugh.

Not so funny was the way he treated Herb Cain, a man in the twilight of his career, but still with some tread left on his tires. Ross had received offers from the Rangers and Black Hawks to buy up the contract of the 33 year old Cain and put him on their rosters. Ross would hear none of it. He kept Cain in the fold, but demoted him to Hershey of the American Hockey League. To Cain, it was a punch to the solar plexus. The NHL pension had just come in, and Cain, with his years of experience, would have been eligible if he could put in one more year with the Bruins. Ross dug his heels in. He was reluctant to dress a guy in his 30s on his big league roster, but just as iffy about dishing him off to another team that might enable Cain to come back and haunt him.

He may have come off looking the heavy, but general managers had that hammer, and Ross barked at Cain, "You're finished in the NHL."

The money Adams used to pay his players was not his, but this wasn't generally known. Hockey historians have uncovered that the Boston owner was in hock for many years to "Big Jim" Norris, grain magnate, owner of the Detroit Red Wings, a large investor in Madison Square Garden, and, through his son, controlling shareholder in the Chicago Black Hawks. Norris had underwritten a series of mortgages that Adams couldn't repay in the earliest and darkest years of the depression. That meant that Norris controlled three out of six NHL clubs, with a fourth, Boston, beholden to him. Under Norris' thumb, Adams couldn't always spring for the players he knew Ross needed. What makes Art Ross's story truly an amazing one is that he managed to cobble together a competitive line-up consisting of Milt Schmidt, Bobby Bauer, Woody Dumart, Bill Cowley, Frankie Brimsek, Roy Conacher, and Flash Hollett, during the shoestring 1930s.

The financial situation in Boston sparked tensions at league meetings, particularly between Ross and Conn Smythe. Their long-running feud was much on the order of Fred Allen and Jack Benny, except that Smythe and Ross meant it, and not just for promotional value. Smythe called Ross one of the most devious men he'd ever met and added that "wherever we met, we fought."

Once, after a particularly dull game in Toronto between the Leafs and Bruins, Smythe countered by placing an ad in the Boston papers, imploring fans who were "tired of the kind of hockey the Boston Bruins were playing," to attend that night's game against "a real hockey club, the Toronto Maple Leafs."

Ross went ballistic and called on the league to fine Smythe. However, Art had the last laugh, for the Bruins won that night, and the crowd was the biggest the venerable Boston Garden had seen all year.

Later, Ross wailed to NHL President Frank Calder about Smythe's language during a game. He brandished a letter

Art Ross

from a priest sitting near the Toronto boss to substantiate his claim that Conn was ruining the league's image with his four-letter vocabulary. Complaints like that were brushed aside, but it was an example of how deep the feeling was between the two men.

One night, soon after Art recovered from a painful hemorrhoid operation, the Leafs came to town. Before the game, King Clancy skated across the ice to present the Boston boss with a dozen roses. It was ostensibly a peace offering, but there was a greeting card from Smythe. The card suggested in Latin that Ross "insert these up your you-know-where." Ross, unversed in Latin, accepted the flowers with a smile. Then he passed them along to a wealthy lady friend, who, unfortunately, did understand Latin.

A truce was called years later when a deadlier and more consequential fracas broke out in Europe. Smythe learned that Ross had two sons in the RCAF fighting that war. By chance, Conn encountered Art with one of those sons, who happened to be in uniform that day. Smythe asked that a picture of the three men be taken, and relations between the two old hardheads gradually grew more cordial.

Arthur Howie Ross was born in the town of Naughton in northern Ontario in January 1886. He first took up the game of hockey as a youth on nearby Whitefish Bay. He made his first big splash as a player with the Westmount team in the Canadian Amateur League. A year later, young Ross became one of the game's first great free agents. He landed in Kenora in time to help the Thistles topple the Montreal Wanderers for the Stanley Cup. The Wanderers then scooped up the rushing defenceman to win back the Cup and fend off challenges from Winnipeg, Toronto, and Edmonton.

It was after a brief stint with the Haileybury franchise in the short-lived National Hockey Association that Art Ross returned to the Wanderers, whereupon he helped lead a players' mutiny for a better share of the revenues from the club owners. He enjoyed brief spells with Ottawa, in which he employed the close-checking defensive style of hockey that stifled free-wheeling enemy attackers. He then returned to Montreal to close out his playing career with the Wanderers in 1918.

Art Ross first took on coaching in Hamilton with the senior A Tigers. At the same time, he served as an NHL official, working a Stanley Cup game in Montreal in 1924. There, he caught the attention of an interested observer named Charles F. Adams, who had just purchased an NHL franchise for Boston. Afterwards, the two men talked and were mutually impressed.

Adams later spoke to a reporter about Ross. "He knows the game and everybody in it. He's got courage, too. He's just the man to manage the Bruins."

Art Ross stayed in the Massachusetts capital, as coach or manager or both, for 30 years. It was a situation for which Ross found himself ideally suited.

"Tough and brainy," Milt Schmidt recalled. "He didn't teach too much, so far as fundamentals were concerned, but he was brainy behind the bench, outwitting the opposition, line changes, etc. And, of course, at contract time he was tough. He didn't have to play second fiddle to anybody."

One rule Ross insisted on in the early going made his players question the "brainy" part of that analysis. He would fine any of his defencemen who took a shot on goal, stressing that the rearguard's role was protect the goalie and feed the forwards for *them* to rush up the ice and score. In time, he came to his senses and relaxed the rule. Eddie Shore was glad; it enabled him to score 105 goals, 12 of them in one season, which was unheard of for a defenceman.

Ross bore out Adams' initial optimism that hockey would go over well in the "Hub." Before long, the Boston Arena the Bruins called home proved too small for the crowds the team was drawing. By the time the Bruins had checked into the spanking-new Boston Garden in 1928, it was ready for the rest of the league as well. The Bruins had a first-class line-up consisting of Tiny Thompson in goal, Eddie Shore and Lionel Hitchman on defence, while Ralph "Cooney" Weiland joined Dit Clapper and Dutch Gainor to form a threesome known as the Dynamite Line. Clapper proved a deadly scorer, while Weiland made his name as a penalty-killing specialist who could also find the back of the net.

Together, Boston won 26 of 44 games that 1928–1929 season, finishing two points behind Montreal in the standings, but drawing the Habs in the first round. The Bruins swept Morenz, Joliat, Hainsworth, and company in three games. Then they turned back the defending champion Rangers in two games for Boston's first taste of Stanley Cup champagne, Thompson shining brightest with three playoff shut-outs.

A lavish victory party was held at the Copley Plaza Hotel, where Adams divvied out $35,000 in bonus money, and GM Ross, whose present was a set of golf clubs, commented that there had been "less bickering, fewer jealousies, and better spirit" on that Bruin squad than on any professional team he'd been involved with. He especially paid tribute to Hitchman as "a cornerstone of the franchise."

Through the 1920s and 1930s, Ross took the coaching reins himself at various times. Then he dished the job off to other men when doing both jobs got to be too much. Cy Denneny directed the Stanley Cup run in 1929 and Weiland in 1941. Frank Patrick, Lester's brother, also had a term behind the Bruin bench in the mid-1930s.

Ross did not carry a whip in his hands when running the practices. He trusted that his men knew how to play the game, and he would even interject some humour into the between-game scrimmages. Milt Schmidt related that one year Ross and defenceman Eddie Shore clashed over the kind of stick Shore was using.

"Everybody had to use a certain type of stick, and it was not the right kind, as far as Shore was concerned. So, [Ross] and Clapper got together, one practice, before Eddie got to the dressing room, they sawed off all of Eddie's sticks, three-quarters of the way through. And, obviously, when Eddie would be shooting or checking, they'd break, so he'd go over and get another one. Finally, after about three or four these broke, he realized that they'd been sawed by somebody, and needless to say, Eddie was very, very upset. But Ross, Clapper, and the rest of us got quite a jolt out of it."

The proud Shore and his boss were not the best of pals. They did battle regularly at contract time, and beyond that, they seldom spoke to one another, functioning independently, yet successfully. Ironically, Ross went on record as saying he didn't think Shore belonged on the Bruins, despite a storied career in the Western Hockey League. He had to be convinced otherwise, and Shore rewarded him and the Bruins with a Hall of Fame career. However, several of Shore's antics almost caused his general manager to blow a gasket.

Ross had a ringside seat on that awful December night in 1933 when his Bruins were hosting Toronto at Boston Garden. King Clancy had just ended a Shore rush into the Leaf end with a trip, and Shore got to his feet with payback on his mind. Probably mistaking forward Ace Bailey for Clancy, or just anxious to flatten anyone in a blue shirt, Shore rear-ended Bailey, sending him into a somersault. The Leafs player's head crashed into the ice. Toronto rearguard, Red Horner, saw this, skated up to Shore, spun him around by the shoulders, and laid him out with a right to the jaw. Both stricken players were taken off the ice, where Bailey started convulsing. Only delicate brain surgery saved his life, but his career was over. A near-riot ensued in which Smythe punched a fan.

Back in Toronto, Bailey's father vowed to shoot Shore. Leafs management had to hire someone to shadow the elder Bailey across the border and keep him plied with booze to prevent him from using his weapon. Meanwhile, Eddie Shore's head required several stitches. He left for Bermuda after learning he had been suspended for 16 games. Without their star, the Bruins lost much of their spark and finished dead last that season. It also inflamed Toronto – Boston passions that much further.

In the off-season, and not for the last time, Ross went off in search of ways to trade his star or sell his contract, but other clubs found Shore's contract too rich.

During one of Art's hiatuses from coaching, Shore's temper again got him into trouble. In the 1936 playoffs, the Bruins had run up a four-goal lead on Toronto in the two-game total-goal series. In the second game at Maple Leaf Gardens, Shore was right miffed at the officiating, and Clancy saw an opening. On the ice, Clancy needled Shore about what a raw deal referee Odie Cleghorn appeared to be giving the Bruins and repeatedly challenged Shore to do something about it. Finally, goaded beyond endurance, Shore fired the puck at Cleghorn, drawing 10 minutes for his troubles. The Leafs took charge, erased the four-goal deficit, and won the series on aggregate, something that could not have endeared Shore to his general manager.

Then there was the night Shore missed the train for Montreal, and had to commandeer a car from some wealthy friends. He drove through a snowstorm and made it to the Forum half an hour before game time. Though suffering from frostbite and exhaustion, Shore played the whole game, except for a two-minute penalty, and scored the game's only goal. Ross was livid, but he fined his star "only" $500.

Finally, in 1940, Ross found he had had enough of

Shore's antics, his individual tendencies, and his contract demands. Ross dealt Shore off to the New York Americans that year, where the brilliant defenceman ended his NHL career.

One school of thought holds that a coach leaves his star alone to play his game, but gangs up on marginal players — "whipping boys," if you will — to get them going. Schmidt could not recollect anyone who fell into that category for Art Ross.

"By and large," Schmidt said, "Ross got along with his players — Clapper, Weiland, and me. If somebody was goofing off, he found other ways to get it out of them," like a glare with that "bad eye."

Ross found ways to get more out of the game as well. He devised a goal net with a B-shaped back to replace the flat-backed nets prevalent until the 1920s, which used to allow pucks to bounce back out again. The "Art Ross Frame" remained the standard for hockey nets until the mid-1980s. He also devised a "bevel-edged" puck, still a staple of NHL play. He pioneered protective helmets and a guard on the back of skate boots to protect against Achilles tendon injuries. Schmidt recalled that Ross usually had a puck in his hand on the bench during games, and later on, a stick that he would use to rap on the boards to indicate when shifts ended. Woe betide the players who didn't obey that signal!

Abraham Lincoln told his Union troops in the American Civil War, "When you are in the field, you are the Union." Great coaches impart that sense of responsibility, that once the puck is dropped, the game is in the player's hands and is effectively out of the coach's hands. Scotty Bowman was enormously successful in making that point clear to his teams in five different cities. Ross, for all his forbidding, laconic nature, possessed that same skill during his years in Boston.

Another knack Ross possessed was to know at what position to assign a man. "The two biggest examples are Dit Clapper, who was a right winger, whom Ross moved back to defence," said Schmidt, "and he did very well behind the blue line, and it extended his career by two or three years. The next example that comes to mind is Woody Dumart, my line-mate (and boyhood chum), who was a defenceman in junior hockey, and when he went to Bruins camp, Ross moved him up to the forward line, and that was how the Kraut Line was formed, with Bobby Bauer on the right side and Woody Dumart on the left."

It was that skill and others that made the 1938–1939 season such a special experience for those who played on that Boston side. Schmidt, who had come of age at 21, was a budding star with the Bruins, scoring 15 goals and 32 points. Ross wanted to sit him out of a late season encounter against the Red Wings, out of fear the youngster would be hurt and unavailable for the playoffs. However, Schmidt was also developing a reputation as a tough guy, and a skill guy, and he would have none of that.

"I'd had something of a running battle with 'Black Jack' Stewart, a defenceman with Detroit. I begged him not to bench me, because the word would get around and that wouldn't do my reputation any good. I said, let me take care of myself out on that ice, and I'll be all right."

Schmidt reinforced how Ross specialized in matching lines, to get his best out on the ice to neutralize the opposition's best, or to keep the opposition off-balance. "One of the games I do remember, against Detroit, is that Ross had me, Bobby [Bauer], and Woody [Dumart] on the bench. And Jack Adams, coach of Detroit, wanted to play line against line. But by benching us, Ross kept their big line off the ice as well. If I remember, we won that game. Those are things that Art Ross would do. But we knew that by benching us, when he didn't want to, he was helping the team. And he thought our other two lines were equal to or better than Detroit's."

In that 1938–1939 season, Ross' line-matching genius came to the fore, as his Bruins won 36 of 48 games and rolled into the final series against the Patrick-led New York Rangers. What else worked to Ross's advantage was that Lester Patrick had let a promising, if not sizable, forward slip away. This slip would come back to haunt him. As mentioned earlier, the youngster, Mel Hill, lit up the Rangers for three overtime goals to give the Bruins the victory. It was Ross's only Cup behind the bench, and despite a couple of years of running the practices and motivating the players, the strain was starting to get to him.

"He was getting up there in years when we won in '38–39," says Milt Schmidt of his then 53 year old mentor, "and it was there that he started to put more of his thoughts into signing the players and putting the team together rather than running it."

Art Ross' final fling behind the Bruins bench was hampered by the depletion of his roster by the war. Some of his men, including Schmidt, Dumart, and Bauer, tried on other uniforms. However, the line-up he was left with included some hungry youngsters like 17 year old Bep Guidolin, who joined with Bill Shill and Don Gallinger to become the Sprout Line. Bep and his mates led the Beantowners to a second-place finish in 1943 and a berth in the Stanley Cup final, before falling in four straight to a determined Detroit squad. In the summer of 1945, Ross finally handed the coaching reins over to Clapper and concentrated on trading, drafting, and hiring full-time.

Shortly afterwards, the tributes began coming Art Ross's way for all his years of service to the game. A new Hockey Hall of Fame, whose physical home was still years from construction, recognized him among its first wave of inductees in 1945. The scoring championship trophy was named in his honour in 1947, and many of his innovations were recognized. He held on as general manager of the Boston Bruins until 1954 and then quietly bowed out. Over 30 years at the helm of the Bruins, the club had finished at the top of the league standings 10 times and captured the Stanley Cup on three occasions in Boston to go with all those championships he had won as a player. Arthur Howie Ross died on August 5, 1964.

Several of the players Ross nurtured and developed became coaches. Milt Schmidt was one of them. Schmidt patrolled the bench starting in the mid-1950s and remained at the wheel until 1966, whereupon he became general manager. It was in that post that Schmidt made some historic moves of his own. He drafted a phenomenon named Bobby Orr; acquired a goalie named Gerry Cheevers; and worked deals to grab Phil Esposito, Ken Hodge, and Fred Stanfield; forming the nucleus of what would become a Stanley Cup champion team twice over, in Boston. Having seen first-hand how Ross ran the show, Schmidt incorporated many of those methods into his repertoire as coach, along with others that suited his own personality.

"Well, besides his being very severe at times, he had a great sense of humour, and I tried to get along with that. I tried to be very stern in the dressing room, in my pep talks, which he never ever made. When the game started, the moves Art Ross made I always believed to be the correct moves. Any move that I made, I'd think, well, Art Ross did it this way, and he thought it 100 percent proper, so I'm going to think that way myself, and nine times out of 10 it worked out fine.

"He had a great mind; I don't think there was any greater mind in hockey than Art Ross."

Chapter 3
Dick Irvin:
The Saviour

C harley Goldman, who trained the unde-
feated heavyweight champion Rocky
Marciano, once explained the mayhem
that overtook his camp when the "Brockton Blockbuster" was
in training for any of his 49 fights. Charley told a reporter that
his fighter didn't know how to ease up on anybody, be he an
unknown sparring partner trying to make it big in the fight
game, or Ezzard Charles trying to take Rocky's title.

"Maybe if he learnt to coast in camp, he'd coast in the
ring," Charley Goldman said. "So maybe it's better he don't
get taught no coastin'."

Many great hockey players, like great fighters, play the
way they practise. While it's a mistake to invest too much
energy on the practice rink and risk injury, often a player who

practises hard is more likely to keep that chip in place on his shoulder when it matters most. There have been coaches who prefer this attitude to the "play-your-way-into-shape" approach, especially since the great Soviet teams succeeded by stressing conditioning.

Dick Irvin agreed with Charley Goldman. The men trying to earn a spot on Dick Irvin's teams knew this. Residents of Mount Royal where the Canadiens conducted their fall training camps in the 1940s and 1950s knew this. Neighbours would hear the sound of bodies slamming against the rink's boards, maybe voices raised in challenge to a fight, and joke that Canada was being invaded. No, they'd conclude, it was just Dick Irvin deciding who was going to make the Habs for the upcoming NHL season.

One way Irvin would set up this scenario was to skate up to the men who made up "The Punch Line" — Maurice Richard, Elmer Lach, Toe Blake — and other veterans like Doug Harvey or Emile Bouchard, and suggest that there were young bucks at the other end of the rink he was impressed with, who might take the older guys' jobs if they weren't careful. Then Dick would skate back to the rookie end of the rink and suggest that there were spots for only one or two of them on the final roster. He would add if they didn't want to subsist on a minor-league salary, they'd better see if they couldn't knock the Rocket or "Butch" on their behinds.

It may not have done much for the cause of brotherly love, but it did ratchet up the intensity level to where Dick

Irvin wanted it. It also created champions. Dick Irvin went to the Stanley Cup final an incredible 15 times, winning the Cup once in Toronto and three more times in Montreal. He proudly pointed out that his teams scored 4,712 goals and had only 3,984 scored on them. Due to his attention to detail and other qualities, Dick Irvin's coaching career provided the standard by which all coaches to follow were measured.

Though his name was never engraved on the game's holy chalice as a player, the on-ice career of James Dickinson Irvin showed sufficient credentials for induction into the Hockey Hall of Fame, apart from his varied stints as a head coach. Followers of amateur hockey in Canada's West in the early twentieth century remember a forward of deft stick-handling, a cool head, and discipline that kept him out of the penalty box. Among the early highlights of his amateur tenure, there was a 1913 performance worthy of a Frank McGee or a Rocket Richard. As his Winnipeg Monarchs drubbed a capable, but flummoxed, Toronto senior squad 9–1, the 21 year old Irvin registered all nine goals. His one-man-wrecking-crew act even caught the eye of Robert Ripley's people, who wrote and drew up his exploits for their "Believe It or Not" syndicated newspaper feature.

The following year, with war still only months away, Dick Irvin led his Monarchs to the Allan Cup, making them monarchs of Canadian senior hockey, before he heeded the call of king and country into the Canadian Army. As luck would have it, the war ended before young Irvin was sent overseas, and he was able to continue his senior career with teams in Winnipeg and Regina.

As the 1920s dawned, Irvin began his pro career with the Regina Pats of the Patrick brothers' Pacific Coast Hockey League. He moved with the team to Portland, Oregon, where the club was re-christened with the less-than-manly name of the Rosebuds. Whatever the flower on the front of his uniform, Dick continued to find the net 31 times in 30 games in 1925–1926, tying Bill Cook of Saskatoon for the league lead. The following year, the league folded, and Dick Irvin's contract was picked up by Major Fred McLaughlin, a Chicagoan whose ambitions dwarfed his hockey knowledge.

Dick was the first captain of the new Chicago Black Hawks; the name was borrowed from McLaughlin's World War I regiment. He picked up as a scorer from where he had left off on the West Coast, notching 36 points in a 43 game season. Then a powerful check from Red Dutton of the New York Americans the following year left him with a skull fracture. This marked the beginning of the end of his playing career.

When the Hawks held their fall training camp at Notre Dame University in Indiana, something magical happened. It was there that 37 year old Irvin noticed how Knute Rockne put the Fighting Irish football team through its paces. He began to think in terms of coaching as a career alternative.

If it can be said that pressure makes diamonds, the situation with Major McLaughlin surely made Dick Irvin shine. The Major had a my-way-or-the-highway attitude toward the men who ran his hockey club. He discarded them like paper towels, firing two coaches a year over the Hawks' first decade.

Whether he knew what he was getting himself into or not, Dick Irvin assumed the helm of a dispirited Windy City team. They had won only seven games the year before, and he guided them to 24 wins in 1930–1931. The Hawks cleared the hurdles put up by the Leafs and Rangers in the playoff rounds and vaulted into the Stanley Cup final, where they bowed in the maximum five games to Howie Morenz and the Canadiens.

However, for Major McLaughlin, who could have taught the college course Crazy Club Owners 101, with George Steinbrenner and Harold Ballard as prize pupils, it some-how wasn't enough. Just before training camp began for the 1931–1932 campaign, the boss sent his coach a telegram stating baldly that his "services were no longer required." A bewildered Irvin went home to Regina to stew in his own juice, but not for long.

That fall of 1931, something was brewing in Toronto, where the first season in the gleaming new Maple Leaf Gardens was starting off with a whimper. After a loss to the Hawks on opening night, Conn Smythe watched his boys go into a tailspin through most of November, winless in their next four, and swooning to dead last in the eight-club league. Smythe found he couldn't trade his way out of the basement, so he asked his coach, Art Duncan, what could be done about the situation. When he didn't get a definitive answer, he showed Duncan the door. Within a matter of days, another wire arrived at the Irvin household in Regina, telling him to expect a long distance phone call soon from the rajah of Carlton Street.

"How would you like to coach the Leafs?" exclaimed the voice on the other end of the line.

Irvin answered with a question: "What's wrong with the Leafs?"

"We've got the best team in the world," boasted Smythe. "There's nothing wrong with the Leafs."

"What about Duncan?"

"He's gone. Do you want the job or not?"

A couple of days later, after giving the matter serious thought, Dick Irvin was on his way to Toronto for the next game against Boston. To ease him into the job, Smythe made the line changes that night against the Bruins, while Irvin peered over his shoulder. As the Leafs squandered a 4–1 lead allowing the Bruins to tie, Smythe turned the reins over to Dick for the rest of the game, saying he would know what to do. Conn was right; the Leafs notched their first win that night, 6–5 in overtime.

Dick Irvin had seen how Knute Rockne lit a fire under his Notre Dame football troops. He made a copy of that take-no-prisoners attitude and painted it blue and white. He told Smythe the talent was there, and all they needed was better conditioning. He turned practices into a kind of boot camp until he saw better results.

Nor would his interest prove merely 9 to 5. One afternoon in New York, the new coach took in a Broadway show with forward Andy Blair. The title and plot of the show have been lost to memory, but by gosh, Blair sure learned to finish his checks against Normie Himes of the Americans, for Irvin didn't stop coaching when he left the rink.

Smythe would drop by practice and marvel at Irvin's boot camp and its affect on the players. Over the years, Conn noticed that Irvin would "fall in love" with some of his men, and "wouldn't fire them or even bench them when they started to go bad." However, that first season, Smythe told his biographer, "Dick coached with his head and not his heart."

Taking his cue from Smythe, Irvin might go around the dressing room after a workout and goad men such as Harvey Jackson or Charlie Conacher about their many women friends and extra-curricular activities, or Hap Day about his upcoming marriage and how it affected his play in the playoffs, or King Clancy about rushing the puck like a forward and not getting back in time to finish the check.

Somehow the message got through. With the improved conditioning and more attention to disciplined hockey, the Toronto Maple Leafs won nine of their next 14 games, and the club climbed to the Canadian division lead by the end of calendar 1931. What's more, a new swagger emerged from the Leafs dressing room. It showed itself when Harold Cotton challenged the Bruins bench during a game in Boston. This was a bunch that knew it couldn't be physically pushed around.

Dick Irvin: The Saviour

The Leafs emerged from their November coma to finish the 48-game season with 23 wins. They glided by the Hawks, especially sweet for the recently fired Irvin, and then passed the Montreal Maroons in the preliminary playoff series. They swept the Rangers in what was called the "tennis series," by scores of 6–4, 6–2, 6–4, to take the Stanley Cup — the first for Dick Irvin, Conn Smythe, and Maple Leaf Gardens. Irvin felt vindication and triumph. After all, he'd shown Major McLaughlin the mistake he'd made by letting him go, and Irvin was now on top of the hockey world.

The rest of the 1930s played out with Irvin and the Maple Leafs near the top of the league year after year. They built a nationwide fan base on the voice of Foster Hewitt every Saturday and became fixtures in Canadian homes. Even though his teams made the finals six more times in Irvin's tour of duty, Smythe noticed that the big guns repeatedly failed to come up big when the Cup was on the line. Thus, 1932 was the last Stanley Cup party in Toronto for 10 years.

Given their respective histories, it's hard to imagine the Toronto Maple Leafs as a "have" team, in comparison with the Montreal Canadiens as "have-not." Such was the state of the game, the country, and the economies of both, at the end of the 1930s, when the Habs were teetering on the edge of folding. There was one game played over the Christmas season in Montreal, in 1939, when the Leafs and Canadiens played to only 1,500 people at the Forum. The most heated rivalry in sports appeared to be fading to embers. When the call went out from Montreal for help with reviving a team in serious danger of flatlining, Dick Irvin was given permission by manager Smythe to talk with Canadiens' management. Some controversy surrounds just why he did so; historians have suggested it was because Conn had a genuine interest in maintaining a solid league; maybe he just felt it was time for a change; perhaps Smythe felt secure his Leafs had coaching talent waiting in the wings and could survive; or just perhaps ... it was because Adolf Hitler was overrunning Europe, and, if left unchecked, could render academic the whole question of hockey in Canada, so Smythe's attention was elsewhere.

The younger Dick Irvin, son of the coach, remembered being in tears the night the New York Rangers beat the Leafs at Maple Leaf Gardens to win the Stanley Cup final in 1940, but he remarked in later years how calmly his father took the situation. Then his dad asked something that startled him.

"Do you think you could start cheering for the Montreal Canadiens? I'm going to be their coach."

It was official. Dick Irvin was changing teams, and he would build a dynasty in Montreal. The Canadiens would go from vagabonds to victors, charity cases to champions — Les Glorieux — in less than a decade, and the architect of that wholesale makeover was one James Dickinson Irvin.

Son Dick Irvin, who went on to become a sportscaster and hockey historian, recalled his father's routine when training camp would begin. Seasons were shorter in the

1930s and 1940s, so players went home for the summers. For the Irvin family, of course, this was Regina. As training camp approached, some players who were prairie boys gathered at the Irvin home on Angus Street and clambered into the coach's 1932 Buick for the long drive to camp in either Toronto or Montreal. It was an annual ritual Irvin observed until his final camp in Chicago, the year before he died, and one not likely to be duplicated today.

One of the first things Irvin did on arrival in Montreal was to invoke the name of World War I poet, John McCrae, and have a verse from his poem "In Flanders Fields" inscribed on the locker-room wall: "To you from failing hands we throw the torch, be yours to hold it high." The words had a galvanizing effect on generations of Canadien players for years to follow. These same words moved with the team in 1996 from the Forum to the Molson Centre.

One of a coach's responsibilities is to lay down the law early. Toe Blake was on his way to a Hall of Fame career as a player, but in the summer of 1940, he had spent time in the army reserve and had indulged in some pub crawls with his reserve cronies. His midsection showed the results. Irvin took one look at the excess flesh above Blake's belt and cautioned him, "You're on my team now, but if you look the same next year, don't bother showing up."

The climb back to the summit did not begin in earnest until Irvin spied an odd-looking rookie in 1942: an intense, 160-pound forward who skated with such speed and, at

times, recklessness, that some veterans at the Habs' training camp speculated that he'd be carried out of the rink on
a stretcher if he wasn't more careful. Somebody muttered
that 21-year-old Maurice Richard "took off like a rocket," and
the name stuck. He'd had his wrist and ankle broken as an
up-and-comer, and he broke the ankle again his rookie season with the Canadiens. Irvin looked past the lad's apparent
brittle bones and saw the fire Richard possessed.

A coach will often have to sit newcomers out of games,
and usually, the rookie keeps a stiff upper lip and finds a
suitable place to watch the game. When Irvin broke the news
to young Richard that he wouldn't be playing one night, the
rookie marched out of the locker room, slammed the door
behind him, and went home. That fury at hearing he wouldn't
be playing was something Irvin liked. He successfully talked
general manager Tommy Gorman out of trading the injury-
prone neophyte, predicting that the kid would not only be a
star, but the biggest star in hockey.

Starting in 1943–1944, Rocket Richard proved his coach
right for years to come. One night he stung Irvin's old team,
the Leafs, for all five Montreal goals in a playoff game en
route to the Canadiens' first Stanley Cup. Richard earned
all three stars that night; a legend was being born on Ste.
Catherine Street.

One day the following December, Richard missed the
morning skate after moving into a new house. He arrived
at the Forum that afternoon half-dead and hinted he might

not play much that night. Irvin, while seething that a young player would risk his physical well being that severely, urged the youngster to "give it a try" that night against Detroit. Again, Rocket Richard made his coach look like a genius that night, notching five goals and three assists in a 9–1 pasting of the Red Wings. He earned a place in the NHL record books, and not for the last time!

Irvin had noticed early on the uncanny scoring touch the youth possessed, particularly for goals late in the game. That same year, he teamed him with former Maroon Hector "Toe" Blake, and Elmer Lach, a Saskatchewan boy like Irvin, on the famed Punch Line. With Blake doing the digging and Lach feeding the Rocket scoring opportunities, Richard made a mockery of the old NHL single-season goal-scoring record that year, turning the red light on 50 times in 50 games.

What made Dick Irvin a champion in Montreal was in helping Maurice harness the competitive fires burning within him. Those who remember the Rocket remarked that he was a player "on the edge." The hazard was that playing on the edge risked his going over that edge. Richard's pride as a French-Canadian and prowess as a goal scorer made Richard a target for the rest of his career. It fell to Dick Irvin to see that the "Rocket's red glare" did not lead to bombs bursting into the air. Dick Irvin knew when to goad Richard and when to hold him up and send teammates in to handle the fisticuffs. He got help in that task from Blake, who grew up in Northern Ontario and was fluent in both official languages.

Hatred of losing was probably instilled in Dick Irvin by the pressure exerted from higher up, but also by the lack of job security written into the coach's contract. Even when success followed upon success in Montreal, those closest to Irvin knew to be on their best behaviour after a loss, for their dad allowed that defeat to shoot deep within him. Broadcaster Dick Irvin said he and his siblings wished their father would go straight to the office instead of coming home after his Habs fell short on the score sheet, for the silence around the house was as cold as 100 Canadian winters. Acknowledgments of family members were at a premium for at least 24 hours; three words out of Dad would be an outburst, 10 a filibuster. The oddest thing was that Irvin would likely get to sleep more easily after a loss than a win; just a quick cup of tea and the coach would be out like a light.

Two more Cups followed for Irvin and the Flying Frenchmen in 1946 and 1953, the latter on an overtime goal by Elmer Lach over Lynn Patrick's Boston Bruins. By then, Irvin had a new crop of players to work with: Jean Beliveau, a regal centreman from the Quebec Aces; Jacques Plante, an acrobatic goalie who revolutionized the position; Bernie Geoffrion, whose lethal slapshot earned him the nickname, "Boom-Boom"; Doug Harvey, as steady a defenceman as there was in the game; and finally, Maurice's teenaged brother, Henri, who eventually needed a third hand for all his Stanley Cup rings.

It was in the spring of 1953 that Irvin juggled his lines,

inserting Ken Mosdell into the line-up, along with role players like Calum McKay and rookie Lorne Davis. He also found a place for the nervous rookie, Plante, to whom he barked across a hotel lobby, "You're playing tonight, and you're going to get a shut-out."

The news could not have settled Plante's nerves, but he girded his loins and shut out the Bruins that night, 3–0, fully justifying his coach's confidence.

However, it was Dick Irvin's handling of the Rocket that proved his greatest pride, his biggest headache, and in the end, his undoing. Maurice never took kindly to the digs he took from enemy players, or to what he perceived as the NHL's reluctance to punish the offenders. When Richard took matters into his own hands — and he did so frequently — the result was often a fine.

Coach Irvin did his best to deflect much of the static Richard took on the ice, certainly from the paying customers. While Richard bridled at the taunting he got from fans, Irvin reveled in it. Bostonians found that out one night when they rode Richard and his mentor, shouting "Hey, Uh-vin, where's yer stah?"

At just the right moment late in the game, Richard showed his scoring magic, whereupon Irvin pointing a finger at his top scorer, hollering back at his tormentors, approximating New England dialect, "Thah's my STAH!"

One catastrophic incident in March of 1955 numbered the days for Dick Irvin in Montreal. Maurice had been highsticked by Bruins defenceman Hal Laycoe, and he went off the deep end. He broke two sticks over Laycoe's shoulders, head, and back. When a linesman got between the two, Richard got his hand free and punched the official. To NHL President Clarence Campbell, that was the final straw. The hockey czar suspended the Rocket for the remaining three regular season games and the entire playoff run.

It was Montrealers' turn to erupt. Fans were incensed at the suspension. They were more so when Campbell attended the Habs' next game at the Forum on St. Patrick's Day. Viewing his presence as a challenge, they pelted Campbell, lunged at him, and finally set off smoke bombs, which forced the building to be evacuated. Some fans took their outrage further, smashing cars and windows in a riot that resulted in some 60 arrests. That the game was forfeited to the Red Wings was a mere footnote; French-Canadian pride was wounded. Some historians credit the incident with launching the independence movement in Quebec, a quiet revolution born not so quietly. All this, over a hockey player!

Canadien management pondered all this over that summer of 1955. Dick Irvin could no longer keep the lid on his star, a man he'd stood up for and behind whom he'd thrown his loyalty for 13 years. Seemingly forgotten were all the successes the two men had enjoyed, transforming the Habs from near bankrupt to the greatest machine the game had ever known. Someone was needed who could make Rocket Richard channel his energies into something positive and keep him from self-destructing on the ice, getting penalized and suspended, and hobbling his mates' Cup chances. The head honchos at the Montreal Forum tried to kick Dick Irvin upstairs to a front office job, in favour of Toe Blake, who'd been coaching in Montreal's farm system. Irvin said no and departed for greener pastures.

Then a call came in from an unlikely source: the Chicago Black Hawks. The meddlesome Major McLaughlin was long since dead and gone, but the franchise he founded was floundering on the ice. In fact, one player called it "the Siberia of the NHL." The Black Hawks were fighting to get fannies back into the seats at Chicago Stadium, and they needed help in the worst way. The club opened up the vault for the four-time Cup winner and paid him a salary of $20,000 a season. This put Irvin at the top of the Hawks' payroll. It was an offer he could not pass up, as in the early 1930s, Dick Irvin was not to find himself idle for long. Chicago was a new lease on life for him and his coaching career. The sparkle in his eyes returned.

Unfortunately, all that money in Dick's bank account couldn't mask the fact that the players he had to work with were not up to snuff and would not be for years to come. The 1955–1956 season wasn't a repeat of 25 years before. The team from the City of the Big Shoulders bowed their heads well below .500 and watched cobwebs form in the NHL dungeon.

This Chicago management proved more lenient than the last time and granted Irvin more time to build a winner.

His health was not so forgiving. Cancer was already attacking his bones as training camp was getting underway in the fall of 1956. Rookies to the Black Hawk camp found assistant coaches putting them through their paces, as Irvin, wrapped up in blankets, peered down at them from the stands, looking at how they skated and how they applied themselves to the practice. Illness had so ravaged his body that he was able to say or do very little.

Finally, one day, before Black Hawk players old and new hit the ice for their morning scrimmage, a stricken Dick Irvin shuffled into the dressing room. He told his charges that as he had always expected 100 percent from them, he had asked the same of himself, but he couldn't give it anymore. The message hit like a sledgehammer; Dick Irvin would no longer be their coach, and he was going home. The tears flowed in that dressing room, some from the coach's own eyes. The man who had helped save hockey in Montreal died there on May 16, 1957, at age 64.

James Dickinson Irvin knew he was good at what he did. His record spoke for itself: eight first-place finishes, four Stanley Cups, 15 appearances in the finals, only twice missing the playoffs in 26 years, 690 wins, third on the all-time list behind only Scotty Bowman and Al Arbour. Not counted in that win total were the knock down, drag-'em-out, intra-squad games played during the last few days of his training camps, games that were often more entertaining to watch than those during the regular season, in camps that forged winners.

Dick Irvin: The Saviour

When he was asked why he turned up the volume full blast in camp, Irvin replied, "It may sound mean, it may sound brutal, but it seemed to work. Some kids earned their ticket to the NHL by busting their arse in that final day of camp."

They earned that ticket because Dick Irvin punched it, and together, they carried the torch that burns bright in the hearts of hockey fans everywhere, to this day.

Chapter 4
Clarence "Hap" Day:
The Unflappable

I t was the last thing fans of the Toronto Maple Leafs needed to hear. Their heroes had their backs to the wall, trailing three games to zip to Jack Adams' Detroit Red Wings in yet another Stanley Cup final in the spring of 1942. Worse, the enemy was throwing the idea of puck control out the window, in favour of a dump-and-chase style that seemed to have the older and slower Leafs players befuddled. It seemed every time someone in blue and white turned around, there was someone in a red uniform ready to pounce on him, pick up a loose puck, and pop it into the Toronto cage. It was ugly to watch, but it seemed to be working for the Motowners, who swept the first two games in Toronto, 3–2 and 4–2. Then they added insult by taking game three in Detroit, at 5–2.

Clarence "Hap" Day: The Unflappable

The news from overseas wasn't getting any better. Hitler's forces had gobbled up most of Europe and were pressing to overtake the Soviet Union. His "wolf packs" had laid waste to tonnes of Allied shipping crossing the Atlantic, and although Britain continued to stand the Fuhrer off, major victories for the Allies were still in the future. In another theatre of the war, the Japanese looked unstoppable after the attack on Pearl Harbour, and Canadians were being marched off to prison camps in Hong Kong and elsewhere in the Pacific.

All signs in the real world pointed to catastrophe and collapse, and the Leafs should have been taking people away from worrying about the war. Frankly, they weren't doing a very good job of it. After eliminating the Rangers in a six-game semifinal, the Leafs had one shoulder on the mat against a hungry Detroit team that seemed to have their number. Their coach had to act, or his team's season would end before the boys knew what had hit them.

With head honcho, Conn Smythe, away fighting that war, Hap Day went to the Leafs' board and told them flatly he was benching regulars Gordie Drillon and defenceman, Bucko McDonald. He had decided to slot in Don Metz and Ernie Dickens, a pair of speedier youngsters who could possibly fend off the Wings' suffocating forechecking.

Then Day went the emotional route with his players. Before game four in Detroit, he took out a letter from a 14 year old girl who said she still had faith in the Leafs and was certain they'd come back. Day read the letter with such conviction that his veterans were galvanized into action and got third-period goals from Syl Apps and Don Metz for a 4–3 victory. The series was far from over, and the drama was just beginning.

Referee Mel Harwood charged Red Wing forward Eddie Wares with talking to him off-colour during the third frame and assessed him with a misconduct. When Wares refused to go to the box, the Wings were given a bench minor. Harwood ordered linemate Don Grosso to serve it for them. Grosso responded by throwing his stick and gloves at Harwood's feet. When the final buzzer sounded that night at the Detroit Olympia, Grosso, Wares, and coach Jack Adams tore after Harwood in protest. Finally, Adams put his fist up and clocked the official one. "Genial Jawn," as he was called, was suspended for the rest of the series, which appeared to unhinge some of his players.

The next time the Wings visited Maple Leaf Gardens, they were not the same swaggering bunch they'd been. They were bombed 9–3 in game five. Their scoring was neutered by Turk Broda, who came up massively in game six back in Detroit, shutting down the Wings 3–0. The Leafs were on the porch of their first Stanley Cup championship in 10 years, after looking all but paralyzed for a good week! After a slew of fractured ankles, the Leafs bandwagon was taking on passengers again.

On that Saturday night, April 18, 1942, the attention of the country was focused, not on the street-to-street battles in Stalingrad, nor on the Japanese invasion of the Philippines, nor on how to stop Rommel in North Africa, but on a group of hardy hockey players who were taking their fortunes into their own hands and turning the tide from defeat into victory. It was a night of no small occasion; even Major Smythe obtained leave to come back to Toronto for game seven, along with more than 16,000 excited fans, a larger crowd than had ever attended a hockey game in Canadian history!

Hap Day was in the driver's seat, and he knew it. As the third period dawned, he called for one more miracle from his enthused troops to bring the Cup home. Only 20 minutes, and Syd Howe's second-period marker, which had given the Detroiters a 1–0 lead, stood in their way.

Wings player, Jimmy Orlando, helped provide the Leafs with their opening about five minutes in, by dumping Apps and creating a power play on which Sweeney Schriner notched the equalizer. Then Pete Langelle converted passes from Bob Goldham and Billy "The Kid" Taylor to beat Johnny Mowers for the go-ahead goal. Schriner got into the act again, potting the insurance goal in the dying minutes. Final score, Leafs 3, Wings 1, and the Cup was back in Toronto.

General pandemonium reigned on Carlton Street. According to the *Toronto Star*, Day hopped over the boards like an acrobat, sought out his forward Schriner, threw an arm around him, and playfully nicked him on the cheek with his fist.

"Hello, Champ," said Day.

"Champ yourself," the giddy Schriner bellowed back above the din of 16,000 delirious fans.

Captain Apps hollered for Major Smythe, who was wearing his military uniform and carrying his riding crop in one hand, "Come on out, Conn. You waited long enough for this Cup. Come and get it."

It is a photograph near and dear to Leafs fans everywhere, a moment frozen in time: Smythe, staring bug-eyed at the trophy that, to modern eyes, looks quite short and skinny in the hands of NHL President Frank Calder; an exhausted Apps grinning ear to ear; and his coach, the architect of that victory, standing proper in a three-piece suit, looking calm and almost above it all.

It was a moment almost 20 years in the making, and yet, it almost didn't happen. Clarence Day, nicknamed "Happy" for his sunny disposition, was of a generation of scholar-athletes not immediately inclined to use athletic skills to make a living. Born in Owen Sound, Ontario, in 1901, he excelled as a senior player in Hamilton before enrolling in the pharmacy program at the University of Toronto, which also involved a playing stint with the Varsity Blues.

The youngster soon caught the attention of Toronto St. Pats manager, Charlie Querrie, who tried to talk him into joining the NHL club. Day wasn't so sure. He informed Querrie that he had his sights set on becoming a pharmacist full-time and opening up his own store someday. The Pats' boss, who seldom took no for an answer, tried a different tack. He suggested young Day could make $50,000 over 10 years as a pro hockey player, open his own drug store, hire someone to run it for him during the season, and have something to retire to after hockey. The prospect of drawing that much money "just on the side" made Hap's head swim, and soon he was trying on the green and white of the Toronto St. Pats. (Conn Smythe bought the franchise two years later, rechristened it the Maple Leafs, and changed the team colours to blue and white.)

Hap made his pro debut on December 10, 1924, on the left wing with Babe Dye and future nemesis, Jack Adams, as his linemates. The following year, Hap was shifted to defence, where he remained the rest of his career. Even on defence, Day became the first Leafs player to record a hat trick. He scored these goals against the Rangers in 1928. He also had a five-point performance, including four goals, against the Pittsburgh Pirates in 1929. He ended up with only 86 goals in his 14-year NHL career, but there was no question of the leadership qualities that initially attracted Querrie.

When the captaincy of the newly renamed Maple Leafs was vacant, there was also no question of who would wear the "C" on his uniform. Hap Day remained captain in Toronto for 10 years. In fact, he became the only man to serve as captain, head coach, and general manager of the franchise in all its history. During his playing career, he made good on his other career goal, when he opened a pharmacy inside Maple Leaf Gardens.

Day's career was kicked up another notch when Conn Smythe won a bet on one of his horses, acquiring the $35,000 needed to lure King Clancy away from Ottawa. Starting in

1931, Hap and King were paired on the Leafs blue line, and they remained there for years to come.

Day broke into goal scoring mode again during the 1932 Stanley Cup playoffs. He tallied on an end-to-end rush to send a second-round game against the Maroons into over-time. Teammate Bob Gracie put the puck in the net to send the Leafs into the final with the Rangers. Day then scored three goals in the first two games of that best-of-five final, in which Toronto triumphed 6–4 and 6–2. Another 6–4 win in game three completed the sweep and gave the Leafs their first Cup.

Day was able to walk away from playing, knowing that he had other irons in the fire. He kept himself busy by offi-ciating at some Leafs home games and worked for Smythe's sand and gravel business. He also decided to take up coach-ing in the minor-league system in Toronto.

In 1936, he coached the West Toronto Nationals in the junior loop, taking the Memorial Cup that year. The next season, he coached the Toronto Dominions to the OHA senior title before losing to the Sudbury Tigers in the pro-vincial championships.

Conn Smythe was watching. The situation in Montreal had deteriorated to the point of near-bankruptcy, and the Leafs were underachieving at playoff time. Conn felt it was time to let Dick Irvin go to Montreal and replace him with Clarence "Hap" Day. A glorious era was about to begin in Leaf Nation.

Day grabbed the reins right away.

"We were meticulously trained," Leafs captain Ted Kennedy said of the system the coach put in place. "It was drilled into us. Day was insistent on doing it his way, leaving as little as possible to chance."

Reporters remarked that Day's training camps more closely resembled prison camps, with the coach clamping down on anyone who made a mistake, most particularly in the defensive zone. They may have cursed him (behind his back, of course) but they learned what they were capable of doing at game time.

Day, having been a defenceman himself, believed in making sure one's check never got away from him. Some opponents complained that the Leafs were nothing but clutch-and-grab artists during Day's tenure, but that style of play proved remarkably effective. Day saw to it that his troops got the puck out of their own zone as quickly as possible. Then they could worry about finding creative new ways to score.

Howie Meeker, who become rookie of the year before his celebrated career as a broadcaster, marvelled that a young player could earn himself a regular shift on the Leafs by knowing what to do in his own end. Once that player got the puck over his own blue line, he was in charge, not the coach. Nearly half a century later, Meeker said that Day was a joy to play for because he never put pressure on his men to score goals, but all the pressure in the world to keep the puck out of their own net. Hockey is a simple game; Day imparted that to his Leafs and prospered for it.

Given the egos of both Smythe and Day, a clash of wills was inevitable. One year, the Leafs boss installed a telephone by the bench, so that Smythe could send instructions to his coach while the game was in progress. Day balked at that practice and had the phone disconnected. This led to a system of couriers, dispatched from Smythe's section up in the third tier to behind the bench. The new coach proved he couldn't be intimidated, which brought him Smythe's considerable respect. After all, the Major insisted to his dying day, if you can't lick 'em in the alley, you'll never beat 'em on the ice, something he applied to life in general, and not just to hockey. Hap Day could hold his own against Smythe, and the players respected that and continued to perform for him.

Day also refused to back down in altercations with officials. He knew the NHL rulebook inside out and could recite obscure rules verbatim, making the men with the whistles roll their eyes. Clearly, he was a force to be reckoned with behind the Leafs bench. Although a Cup eluded him his first season, when his charges dropped a seven-game semifinal to the Boston Bruins, there was no question who was in charge of this club!

When Conn returned from the war, he engaged in moving bodies around to make the team Day coached stronger. He hammered home to his squads that "you can't win this year on what you did last year." He also had an eye on the papers, noticing that it would take more effort to bump football's Argonauts off the front sports pages than in the past. The Double Blue were crafting a dynasty of their own, taking three straight Grey Cups in the years following World War II. Conn knew that a trade or controversial statement would mean more ink for his team, especially during the fall, when the Argos were gathering steam.

Day didn't balk at these attempts to bolster his roster. He knew that the team was defensively sound enough for Smythe to focus on getting a pure scorer. He didn't bat an eye when the Major went to Chicago management with a plan to pry loose NHL scoring king, Max Bentley, from the Black Hawk roster. Day acknowledged that the Leafs had added a third Stanley Cup to his mantle the previous spring by having two of the game's finest face-off men in Kennedy and Apps; a third centre who could also put the puck in the net would be the icing on the cake.

Realizing that Max had enjoyed success in Chicago playing alongside brothers, Doug and Reg, and that the Black Hawks were iffy about breaking up a set, Smythe reckoned that quantity would sweeten the pot, so he offered no fewer than five Leafs for Bentley and a Black Hawk teammate. Some sportswriters thought Conn had lost his marbles in proposing such a risky deal, but on November 2, 1947 — right in the heart of football season — Max Bentley, the "Dipsy-Doodle Dandy from Delisle, Saskatchewan" became a Leafs player. After getting over the shock of no longer working with his brothers, Max starting potting big goals for Toronto and

Tim Horton (centre) and a teammate talk to coach Hap Day.

helping carve Hap Day's name on the Cup once again.

No matter who Conn hired to wear the blue and white, it was Clarence "Hap" Day who was in charge once they threw those proud uniforms on. Howie Meeker, one of his prize pupils, said that players usually got Monday off, having played two weekend games, and that some guys really loved

76

to party. Day knew who the drinkers on his team were, and he would work them all the harder when they got to his practice on Tuesday, hungover or not.

One morning, he called Howie Meeker and woke him up. He asked Meeker where he'd been the night before. Meeker told Day he hadn't been out, as he didn't drink, nor had he been to a movie with his latest date. Well, Day told him, somebody had been driving in Meeker's car — meaning the vehicle had been stolen. The coach somehow knew of the theft before the player did!

Day's 1948 squad, with newbie Bentley registering 23 goals and 48 points, glided through to the playoffs and disposed of Boston in five games before sweeping the Red Wings in four, for their second straight Cup. They completed the "three-peat" in 1949, despite a sub .500 regular season, again downing the Bruins and Wings in only one more than the minimum eight games. The Toronto Maple Leafs made history, just as they had done in 1942. Hap Day had his hands around the Cup for the sixth time, his fifth as a coach and his third in a row.

Day spent one more season behind the Leafs bench before moving upstairs to become assistant general manger. He ran the office and concluded the player deals under Smythe. There was one more Cup celebration for Leafs fans in 1951, under former Day teammate, Joe Primeau.

The decade following that Cup triumph provided something of a trough for the blue and white, as current stars became long in the tooth, fell off their game, and ended up being sent elsewhere. Later in the decade, league owners, led by Smythe, reacted with near paranoia to the prospect of a players' union and clamped down on the idea and its leaders with fury. The ringleaders were sent off to other clubs, tying Day's hands and not working to the betterment of the Toronto Maple Leafs.

Day was never comfortable in the role of assistant GM. His self-esteem took a bruising under all the second-guessing and undermining he took from Smythe.

In 1958, the final straw came, when Day was eased out of his job to make room for Stafford Smythe, Conn's son. Leafs fans gnashed their teeth as the organization began its descent into the abyss, which Cup success in the 1960s only masked.

Day made a clean break from the game, never to return. He purchased a company that produced axe and tool handles, and, in the words of sportswriter Brian McFarlane, "swept those memorable championship seasons almost completely out of his mind."

Day vowed to get out with his dignity. "I was glad to get away from it. I would rather have dug ditches rather than stay with the game." In time, he mended fences with his old boss, Smythe, and their friendship resumed. Day lived to be 88, passing from the scene in the winter of 1990.

Looking back at his record, there is a sense that Clarence "Hap" Day never really needed the game. He got into pro hockey to beef up his bank account while waiting to open his own drugstore. By the time he left, 34 years later, his name was counted among the greatest in the game with a record of success unparalleled in history — Memorial Cup champion coach and Stanley Cup winner as player, coach, and general manager. He may have wanted to forget the aggravation, but hockey fans will never forget how Hap Day led his team from the absolute edge of elimination to Stanley Cup glory, and then, as if to prove it was no fluke, executed the first three-Cup streak in history, providing Leafs fans of the 1930s and 1940s with many fond memories. Those were Toronto's glory years!

Chapter 5
Hector "Toe" Blake:
The Winner

I n the fall of 1967, Hector "Toe" Blake was in his last year as head coach of the Montreal Canadiens with seven Stanley Cups already on his resume, when he found himself on a flight out of Oakland, California. His team had won only one of their last eight games, and the previous night's loss to the Seals was a particularly painful one. To the Bruins, Rangers, or even the hated Maple Leafs, a loss would be torture enough ... but to the California Seals expansion team? To make matters worse, the flight taking the team to its next game in Los Angeles was a bumpy one, and it was quite some time before players, coaches, reporters, and flight crew could count themselves out of danger.

Finally, the plane landed in L.A., and the players breathed

a sigh of relief and waited for their bags and transport to the hotel. Toe Blake, still in his "losing game" personality, was standing off to the side, keeping his distance from his players, staring at the ground, and not uttering a peep.

To break the ice, one Montreal reporter sidled over and asked Toe, "Rough flight, Coach, wasn't it?"

Blake was never a fan of talking to scribes under the best of circumstances. He kept his gaze on the baggage room floor tiles and snarled, "I wish the ****ing thing had crashed."

Believers in reincarnation would probably not want to come back as Toe Blake's bathroom mirror, particularly the morning after a loss. The look that the Canadiens coach would give that mirror could provide a horror show with an image to rival anything imagined by Stephen King or Bram Stoker. Blake hated to lose and didn't care who knew it. He told reporters it wasn't in his nature to swallow a loss affably, and that when he learned to do so, he'd quit. Blake knew that his predecessor, Dick Irvin, had created an atmosphere where winning was expected, and the pressure to maintain that level of play every year was enormous.

The younger Dick Irvin, who ultimately graduated from being the coach's son to top hockey commentator and source authority on the game's history, brushed up against this side of Blake's personality on several occasions. One of his career stops along the way was as official scorer at Canadien home games at the Forum. He would gather up his night's work, recount the goals, assists, and penalties, present the stats sheets to the visiting coaches first, and then head to the Montreal dressing room. Irvin found to his amazement that after the visiting team lost, the other coaches didn't seem all that upset. However, on those rare occasions when the Canadiens lost at home, Irvin dreaded the trip to the Hab locker room. There he would find Toe Blake on the edge of a table in the middle of the room, fedora tilted back on his head, eyes blazing, and, most often, staring at the floor. Everything said was spoken in whispers. Irvin would present Blake with the stats sheet and nip off, without so much as a thank-you from the bench boss.

For Toe Blake, the job of coaching was an emotional grind, one that didn't get easier with the years. He would almost weep after a win, just as he would weep after a loss. He was good on the blackboard with explaining the pre-game strategy. He could also be an emotional leader. In time, the villain known as Alzheimer's disease took away his memory of the wins, and mercifully, also the losses, but it also took away everything else in his career and life. At his best, as player and coach, Toe Blake achieved the summit of the sport, in what many acknowledge to be the golden age of the NHL. He was, to quote sportswriter Red Fisher, "a kindly old coach, a gentleman, and a son-of-a-bitch, all in the same sentence."

Blake was also one of those few men who leapt right into coaching ranks without missing a beat. He kept stars on their game without letup; he just seemed to know when they were rolling and when they weren't. He didn't make the mistake of some players who take the coach's role and insist on casting their employees in their image, notably NBA great Bill Russell ("I tried to treat my players like me, and some of them weren't") and CFL icon Russ Jackson, sacked after two dismal seasons at the helm of the "Good Ship Argo."

Too often these days, fans watch players fire clearing passes cross-ice in their own zone, frequently a recipe for disaster. Toe Blake, a firm believer in keeping it simple, would never abide that. He stressed relentlessly that the puck travelled in two directions: one away from your net, the other toward the other team's net. His insistence on keeping it simple might put him at odds with forwards of today who value creativity, but the consensus of hockey historians is that Blake would find a way to handle them, too.

Fortunately for his blood pressure, Blake won a whole lot more than he lost, taking Stanley Cups in each of his first five seasons behind the bench of the Montreal Canadiens. This put him into the rare company of coaches/managers who became champions before they grew comfortable in their own offices, and stayed champions long after, much like Casey Stengel (whose Yankees were World Series winners in his first five years as manager) and Hugh Campbell (who won Grey Cups in each of his first five campaigns piloting the Edmonton Eskimos).

More than that, Blake would take an outlaw of a player and turn him into a statesman, clash with a goaltender who revolutionized the position, and countenance drunks and other eccentrics. In so doing, he created a mix that turned intermittent success in Montreal into an unbroken string.

Hector Blake was born in 1912 in a now-vanished mining town called Victoria Mines in the Sudbury, Ontario area. He began his journey up hockey's Everest in the early 1930s, ironically enough, at Maple Leaf Gardens. Blake had just had an OHA senior championship season with the Hamilton Tigers. After a Leafs game, he approached Conn Smythe to express his interest in donning a Leafs uniform in the near future. His timing left a bit to be desired. The Leafs had just lost that game, and Smythe was not in a mood for pleasantries, even if a promising amateur star was offering to help. Blake's impromptu job interview went nowhere, and both men went home in a huff.

A few months after that unhappy incident, the Montreal Maroons came calling. The team was only three years away from folding, but it had a solid enough line-up to win the Stanley Cup over Toronto in 1935, with Lionel Conacher, Cy Wentworth, Hooley Smith, and Alex Connell. Because of 23 year old Blake's inexperience, he watched much of that effort from the bench, but he must have chortled at winning the Cup in his first pro season — at Maple Leaf Gardens!

Maroon management decided that Blake needed more seasoning and sent him back to Providence of the Can-Am semi-pro league. There, he flourished under Coach Bert "Battleship" Leduc, so much so that the Canadiens called him up in February 1936. He got into 11 games before finally cracking the starting line-up the next season.

To a squad whose financial situation looked redder than red, white and blue, and who appeared doomed to suffer the same fate as the Maroons, Toe Blake lent a much needed credibility. He began his hardware collection in 1938–1939, leading the NHL in scoring with 47 points and adding the Hart Trophy as the league MVP. It was also the first of his three first team all-star appearances. Toe added the Lady Byng Trophy for sportsmanship and gentlemanly conduct to his mantle in 1946. Curiously, though he would later be put on a line with an injury-prone kid named Richard who could find the back of the net like nobody's business, Toe's other nickname would be "The Old Lamplighter" for *his* goal scoring prowess. His career total was 235, less than half that of the Rocket, but significant nonetheless.

When Blake and Richard had a smooth playmaker from Saskatchewan named Elmer Lach placed between them at centre, they were called the Punch Line. The joke was on the rest of the league, as the threesome and the rest of the Habs started to click, moving smoothly to the Stanley Cup finals in 1944, against Chicago. There was no riding the pine for Toe Blake this time, as he notched the winner in the overtime session of game four to give the Canadiens their first Stanley Cup in 13 years. Two years later, Blake scored a personal best 67 points, while helping Richard become the first 50-goal man in NHL history. In 1946, Blake led all playoff scorers with seven goals in nine games to help bring the team its second sip from Lord Stanley's mug in three years, his third and last as a player.

Blake's final campaign, 1947–1948, was an abbreviated one, cut short by a hard check from a Ranger player that left him with a broken leg. After hanging up his uniform, Blake invaded the coaching ranks, first with the Canadiens' Central League farm team in Houston, then with Valleyfield in the Quebec Senior League, and finally with the Buffalo Bisons in the American Hockey League.

When the time came for Canadiens' senior management to replace Dick Irvin as coach, Toe Blake was definitely a front runner, but his accession to the plum post was anything but a shooin. Blake knew that he was not uppermost in the mind of general manager Frank Selke, who went on record as saying he preferred former Leafs coach Joe Primeau. He was sure "Father Frank," as the boss was nicknamed, viewed Toe as just another carbon copy of the intense, fiery Dick Irvin. In short, Blake knew that Frank Selke was not in his corner.

Much anxiety ran through Toe Blake's nervous system as he saw former teammate Kenny Reardon — then assistant general manager — go to bat for him. Reardon told the Habs' board of directors that one of Irvin's weak points was a perceived lack of sensitivity to French Canadians, Richard being the obvious exception, in the playing and coaching ranks, and that hiring the bilingual Blake would solve at least that problem. Moreover, Reardon knew that Blake knew much of the current Canadien roster that would take the ice that fall of 1955, meaning that the learning curve would not be so steep. These arguments, made by an old teammate, eased the way for Toe Blake to become coach of the Canadiens. A new era of unbroken success was ushered in.

Blake's first look at his new brigade must have made his mouth water. There were both Maurice Richard and younger brother, Henri; Jean Beliveau as centre; hard-nosed forward Dickie Moore; slapshooter Bernie Geoffrion, the previous year's scoring champ; the determined Bert Olmstead; Doug Harvey, a rushing defenceman and just about the best power play quarterback anyone had ever seen; and finally, an eccentric goalie named Jacques Plante, with whom Toe tangled for the next seven years. Together, they comprised an awesome hockey machine that dominated the league for years. They became the Flying Frenchmen of legend … once Blake succeeded in getting Maurice Richard to count to 10, rather than blow a gasket and serve 10!

Blake's Habs were still smarting from having the Cup snatched from their grasp the previous spring, first, by Campbell, and then by Tommy Ivan's Detroit Red Wings. They went at their work with a vengeance, compiling the team's first 100-point season ever and taking first place in the six-team league. Plante, despite all his wanderings from the crease to play the puck, picked up his first Vezina Trophy, while the Rocket dotted the score sheet with 71 points, and brother Henri picked up 40 points. The Montrealers toppled the Rangers in five semifinal games, before turning the finals into the Jean Beliveau show. The regal centre scored seven times as the Canadiens got their revenge on the Red Wings, copping the cup in five games. After what seemed an eternity, Lord Stanley's mug was back in Montreal.

The great Soviet teams turned the heads of hockey fans from the 1960s onward with their brand of hockey, stressing constant movement of players and puck. Such rhapsodizing made Beliveau laugh, for it was that type of game Montreal perfected in their glory years of the 1950s. Toe Blake fostered this style of play; he didn't believe one could or should accept a pass standing along the boards and not moving.

In practice, he would shout at his men, "How can you catch the pass? You've been skating around with your stick around your waist! If you want the pass, keep your stick on the ice."

Hab players were expected to dish the puck off to a teammate, already in motion skating only a few feet away, and then hustle for the return pass from that teammate.

Blake exhibited intolerance for lazy play or poor basics, but as long as one gave his best effort, that player would not find himself in Toe Blake's doghouse. Beliveau expressed the view that Blake got the most out of the team by treating everyone equally "from the Rocket to the rookies," as long as they showed discipline and subordinated ego to what was best for the team. Blake would seldom bawl a player out in front of other people. During games, he would pace back and forth, staring up and talking to the clock, but the players always knew who he was talking to.

The following year, the Canadiens fell short of first place, but they showed their boss they were ready at playoff time. The Rocket, whom many feared was a tad pudgy by then, silenced the critics in game one of the finals against Boston. He potted four goals, as Les Glorieux roared to a second straight title in only five games. The next two seasons, Montreal again occupied the top spot at the end of regular league play. They took Boston in six games in 1958 and Toronto in five contests in 1959.

The amazing story about those last two Cups for Blake and the Habs was that the Rocket was lost to the team much of the time, missing a total of 70 games in those two seasons. Blake was fortunate in having a bevy of talent around him, but he was skilful at keeping those players functioning at such a high level for a long time. He emphasized that the last guy on the bench was just as important as either of the Richards, Beliveau, Geoffrion, or Harvey, as long as he pulled his weight and put the team first.

Gilles Tremblay, later to become a colour commentator on Radio-Canada, was a vital cog in the Blake machine in the 1960s. Tremblay knew that Blake realized it was a long season, and while he insisted on a solid effort from each player, he did not make practices the be-all and end-all the way Irvin or rival Punch Imlach did in Toronto. Thus, players

Toe Blake patrols behind the Canadiens bench.

did not burn out, but maintained a consistent energy level throughout the season.

Tremblay, a skilled checker, was told by Blake, "You're going to have to balance your game. You'll have to score some goals. You'll have to believe me and follow my instructions. I'm going to get on you in practice. I'll give you the whip."

The prospect of the whip during practices may have put the fear of God into the young player, but it worked. Gilles put the biscuit in the basket 32 times during his second season.

Hector "Toe" Blake: The Winner

The last and strangest of the Stanley Cup streak years in Montreal began with an issue regarding his net minder. Toe was driven half out of his mind whenever Jacques Plante strayed out of the crease to play the puck to a teammate. (Now, of course, wandering goaltenders are almost commonplace.) However, Plante generally knew what he was doing, and for all his eccentricities (knitting toques on road trips; staying in a separate hotel from the rest of the team because he was convinced the cleaning solution used at the team's hotel aggravated his asthma), "Jake the Snake," as he was called, delivered the goods. Each of the Cup years of the late 1950s brought another Vezina Trophy for Plante, which mitigated his coach's hard feelings ... a little bit.

"Toe and Jacques had a stormy relationship," Beliveau said later in his autobiography. "Both were very strong personalities unafraid to speak their minds."

Blake always stressed discipline, teamwork, and the equality of every team member. Individualist tendencies rubbed him the wrong way. But Plante was going to be who he was. He was a keen student of the game and the best goalie in the world, so why should he change?

In the fall of 1959, Plante had been experimenting with using a mask in practice. Blake had said that was all right, but not in a game, reckoning it would obstruct his goaltender's vision, especially on shots down around his skates. Suddenly, it seemed Blake was willing to make a bargain with his net minder.

"If you get a puck in the face, then you can wear it," Blake remarked.

Sure enough, on November 1, 1959, at Madison Square Garden, Ranger Andy Bathgate got off a rising shot that cut Jacques' nose and upper lip for seven stitches. It also broke the camel's back, as it were. While his coach and the Madison Square Garden's faithful might have called Plante's guts into question, he was the only goalie the Canadiens had that night. If he was coming back onto Garden ice, it was with facial protection. Blake might have fumed about it, but a deal was a deal, and hockey history was made. (Plante answered his critics with a question: "If you jump out of a plane without a parachute, does that make you brave?")

Call it a case of losing a battle to win the war. Blake hated losing face, but he hated losing games all the more. Montreal beat the Rangers that night, and they posted another nine without a loss. A few weeks later, Plante went barefaced against Detroit and lost. The mask went back on the next night, and it stayed on until Plante's retirement, 15 years later.

The Canadien band of brothers continued with their fast, flowing, and highly integrated team play, as their coach had insisted. They went all the way through the final round against a pesky Toronto team, whose coach, Punch Imlach, told all who would listen that the Leafs would prevail in six games.

Blake refused to get into a predictions battle with his rival. He told reporters, "We'll just go out there and play our best. Besides, predictions are for gypsies."

Blake must have known that the spring of 1960 would be the final bow for Maurice Richard. Then a bit chunkier and no longer his fleet self, the Rocket relied on his steady scoring hand to register his 82nd — and last — post season tally in a game three victory over the Leafs. Plante was predictably in what would prove a four-game sweep, letting just five goals behind him, as the boys of Carlton Street fell again to what Conn Smythe called "the greatest team of all time."

Blake had done it yet again. Under his leadership, the Habs had made the finals 10 years in a row, and they had won the Cup five years in a row. As the Toronto Maple Leafs under Imlach became the dominant power in the early 1960s, the Habs failed to arrive at the big dance four years in a row.

With the Rocket era ended, a clearing of the decks took place in Montreal, as first Harvey, then Plante, then a number of stalwart veterans, were unloaded to the Rangers. New young bucks were brought in: a hardworking centre named Ralph Backstrom; tall, gangly defenceman Jacques Laperriere; and smooth-skating forward Bobby Rousseau. There was also Yvan Cournoyer, a forward with eye popping speed, and a bruising winger, John Ferguson. Blake and general manager Frank Selke collaborated on making the team bigger and stronger, with not only John Ferguson, but Terry Harper, Claude Larose, and Ted Harris.

"Deluxe plumbers," Beliveau called them, in contrast to the "Flying Frenchmen" of the 1950s. It was not meant as a knock, far from it. Believeau said strong guys who bumped opposing players around and made it easier for the scorers to do their thing were just what was needed for the team to win. They did, three more times, starting in 1965.

Whatever had gone wrong in the early 1960s, Blake had not lost his eye for talent. He never asked more of these young guys than they could give. He knew that slumps were par for the course, too. If a player found himself in one, Blake would back him at once and help that player out of it as soon as possible.

It wasn't that he became a nice guy all of a sudden. He still rode certain individuals, especially Ferguson, when he let his check get away. One night against New York, Rod Gilbert got 16 shots on Gump Worsley, who had come in the Plante deal, four of them for goals. Blake had assigned Fergie to cover Rod, but his man ended up in the penalty box too many times to stop the Ranger sniper.

"Toe really gave it to me and it didn't seem to matter that I had all those penalties," Ferguson recalled. "It was all my fault. [But] I'll tell you, whenever we played the Rangers after that I never took my eye off Gilbert, never gave him more than two inches of room."

What John Ferguson remembered most about Toe Blake was that he never forgot anything. "He had a memory like an elephant." He also noted that Blake would get emotional in intermission pep talks and sometimes lose control of what he was saying, "Now I'm not going to mention any names, but Fergie, I want you to check Ronnie Ellis [of

Toronto]. Backstrom, cover Mikita [when we play Chicago]."
But recounted most fondly by the Canadiens' "top cop" was
that Blake had no curfews. The men in *bleu, blanc et rouge* of
Montreal were trusted to police themselves.

Blake often went on his gut instincts with how a game
would go. Beliveau recollected that Blake just knew from the
first shift who would have a good game and who would not,
just from the way they were skating or handling the puck. One
night, for example, Doug Harvey found himself fooling around
with the puck and losing it too often for his coach to swallow.

Blake whispered to Beliveau or Richard, "Look at that.
I'll bet you he'll trip somebody and get a penalty in the next
25 seconds when somebody takes the puck off him."

Sure enough, that's what happened.

With the 1967–1968 season, changes came with which
Toe Blake could not cope. Expansion and the boom in
salaries it brought ate into the coach's authority to impose
discipline, at least the way Blake was used to applying it. It
also brought more travel, more games, more opportunities
to lose, and more stress. Blake must have thought to himself
that this was not the NHL he grew up with, and not one he
wished to stay with much longer.

Certainly, the mid-season slump didn't help his nervous
system. The expansion draft left unprotected such stalwarts as
Charlie Hodge, Leon Rochefort, Dave Balon, Jean-Guy Talbot,
Red Berenson, Jim Roberts, and Noel Picard. Worse, a few
weeks into the season, Beliveau went down with a knee injury,

and by Christmas, the once-proud Montreal Canadiens were dead last in the NHL's Eastern Conference. (Expansion had created two divisions.) In the Montreal dressing room, doubt grew about whether they would even make the playoffs. Doubtless some gripes got louder about how former teammates were cashing in, being on expansion teams.

All the while — whatever he may have been feeling inside — Blake was telling everyone he encountered that the Canadiens would make the playoffs ... and even win them. Time proved him right. When Beliveau returned and caught fire, rookie Jacques Lemaire pitched in with his steady play at centre, and Richard, Rousseau, and Cournoyer started to perk. The Habs went on a tear, winning 28 of their last 38.

In the middle of the playoffs, though, Blake could not keep the torment inside any longer. After his team made mincemeat of the Boston Bruins and Chicago Black Hawks to advance to the Stanley Cup final, Blake summoned Beliveau to his hotel room following a practice one day. Pointing to his head, the coach told his captain that "something's going to snap." Blake told Beliveau that 13 years of having to keep the team shipshape had finally overwhelmed him. This playoff run would be the end of the line.

It was fortunate that the opposition in the final were the St. Louis Blues, rife with experienced bodies, but raw in terms of playoff experience. More than that, the team, coached by old protégé Scotty Bowman, had endured a knock down, drag-'em-out series against Philadelphia and Minnesota, with game seven of the North Stars series going into overtime.

The downside was that the Blues gave Blake and his Habs fits, playing with the heart and spirit that marked Blake's early teams of the 1950s. Montreal swept the series, but each game was decided by a single goal. Game four was a hard-checking affair. Ironically, it was broken up by a defenceman, the man Blake and the boys called "Grumpy," J.C. Tremblay, who notched the game winner in the third. For the eighth time in 13 years, Toe Blake was a Stanley Cup winning coach. What better way to get out ... *on top!*

Toe Blake handed off the reins to Claude Ruel, who was rewarded with another Cup the following year. The age of the Montreal players was showing, and the glory would again take years to replace. It would take another crop of players, and another driven coach, inclined to be a pain in the butt if that's what it took to win. That man's name would be ... Scotty Bowman.

Hector Blake kept in touch with the game through his pub located near the Forum. There, men — for that's all "Toe Blake's" allowed — could wolf Montreal smoked meat sandwiches and wash them down with a draft before heading to the rink to watch another win. Blake knew when to quit, and he knew when to stay out. His record of eight Stanley Cups would eventually fall to Bowman, but not until the next century.

Still, he would wail to all prepared to listen that discipline had fled the game in the modern era. He would tell the younger Dick Irvin, "Your dad couldn't coach today. Punch couldn't coach today, and neither could I." Blake was still as emotional as ever.

Toe Blake seemed to live out the dictum of NFL coach George Allen: when you lose, you die; when you win, you're reborn. Critics may argue that a coach couldn't lose with the talent he was given, but they should be reminded that an NHL season is a marathon, and not a sprint. Keeping a team sharp, even one laden with stars, through a long season and playoff run requires adjustments by the man in charge. Casey Stengel, Hugh Campbell, Vince Lombardi, Red Auerbach, Phil Jackson, all the great coaches of this world know that. Toe Blake knew that. In many respects, he was what the Montreal Canadiens, the Stanley Cup playoffs, the game itself, is all about.

Chapter 6
George "Punch" Imlach: The Warrior

t was the spring of 1966, and if his team was about to fall, George "Punch" Imlach was going to go down fighting. They had dropped their straight to Toe Blake's Montreal team in the first round of the Stanley Cup playoffs, and, in the final period of game four, Punch had seen enough. He had watched his scorers languish and referee Art Skov dish out another power play to Montreal. Imlach was going to take the law into his own hands.

Everyone in Toronto's fabled Maple Leaf Gardens could see what Imlach was up to, all the way to the upper-tier grey seats, and they wondered if he'd truly lost his marbles. Punch had his skates on and was going to step onto Gardens ice and give Skov what for. He knew he risked a fine; he also knew he may have been putting his head on the chopping block, given the friction between him and management. He didn't care. Punch was steamed and determined to go out in spectacular fashion if need be, if it meant lighting a fire under his beaten and discouraged players.

In the end, common sense got the better of the stubborn Imlach, and he stayed where he was. Unfortunately, this attempt to rally the troops fell flat, as they lost 4–1 to the Habs, who completed the sweep. It also conjured up a worrisome question for residents of Leaf Nation, as they pondered an early summer recess: had Punch lost his mind?

Debate still rages as to whether Punch Imlach was a great or even good hockey coach. He scored successes beyond anyone's wildest dreams in two different cities, and one of his teams won four Stanley Cups in all. However, he had critics, some in his own dressing room, who stoutly maintained that his Toronto Maple Leafs should have won more. Others among the press faulted his trading strategy as general manager, which they said undermined his performance as coach. Still others in the hockey world questioned whether Imlach's tactics and employee relations skills belonged to a bygone era — when the game was all that mattered and men followed orders — and wondered if he stayed around too long.

Imlach brought a dormant team back to life in Toronto and made it proud again. He took another from the ground up, more than a decade later, to the brink of Stanley Cup glory. In a span of 30 years, Punch Imlach left his mark on the game of hockey, knowing coaching success at the junior, senior, and pro levels. Whether through his military-style means to motivate his players, the mind games he played with the opposition, his use of resources to bring better talent to his clubs, or just smoke and mirrors … simply put, whatever he did worked. His career provides a truly amazing story.

From an early age, young George Imlach harbored the ambition to be an NHL star. The sight of Maple Leaf Gardens filled the teenager with such awe that after skating a lap around the rink, he lost his lunch over the boards.

No question he loved a good scrap, even if he didn't always win. Once, Imlach was knocked unconscious in a fight. When he came to in the dressing room, he started swinging his fists, as if picking up the fray where he left off. The incident gave the youngster the nickname "Punchy" — which was later shortened to Punch.

Imlach scored some success with the Young Rangers, junior Marlboros, and senior Goodyears, all Toronto-area teams. He may have just been hitting his stride as a player when World War II intervened. Punch enlisted in the service, and his military experience was seen later in his behaviour toward subordinates and rivals. It taught him organization, motivation, and authority. If he could not *be* the star warrior on the hockey team, dazzling teammates and opponents with skill, he could be the general, leading his troops to victory. He projected an aura of command behind the bench. He dressed the part, with a distinctive fedora. He even formed his lips in a Patton-like sneer, to place the fear of God in young players, especially those who had let the side down with a bad pass or penalty. Love him or hate him, Punch was the leader; he let everyone know it, and no one forgot it. Only a handful of years passed before he got his first "tour of duty" as a hockey coach.

After his discharge from the military, Imlach, by then in his late 20s, got an invite to the Detroit Red Wing tryout camp. Incredibly — or perhaps, realistically — Punch passed on the opportunity. He figured his time in the forces, away from the game, had left him overweight and lacking the stamina to withstand a full season. He took a job in the accounting department of Quebec City based Anglo-Canadian Pulp and Paper. Before long, he was at the helm of a company-owned team called the Quebec Aces, as player-coach. Some of his charges included Herb Carnegie, who never got his shot in the NHL (some said because of his colour), and Jean Beliveau, whom Aces' fans wanted to keep forever. Punch stayed with the Aces for 11 years. He moved up to general manager, and even owned a piece of the team, before he shifted to Springfield for one year.

In 1958, Punch Imlach's life turned completely around when he joined the Toronto Maple Leafs as assistant general manager. With strongman Conn Smythe approaching age 65 and relinquishing more and more control of the club to others, a "hockey committee" of several men, including his son Stafford, controlled player contracts. Hence, there was no "general manager" per se. For a team in the hockey wilderness through much of the 1950s, finishing dead last the previous season, "management by committee" was not the answer. Somebody came up with the brainstorm of making head coach Billy Reay the full-fledged general manager as well, but Reay was only interested in coaching. Imlach promptly stepped in to fill the void. He used his newfound clout within weeks to fire Reay and take over the coaching reins himself. Punch appeared to have all bases covered; the general manager's post would give him added influence in the dressing room, power he would wield with relish for the next 11 years.

Punch Imlach valued loyalty and stuck with guys to the bitter end when they had remained loyal to him. When dealing for players, he looked for veterans who could adapt to his style, had been through the wars, and grew in the heat of battle. Younger men were unknown quantities, with minds of their own, and with educational interests outside of hockey. These upstarts were often viewed by Imlach with suspicion. He thought they were more likely to resist the kind of locker room dictatorship Punch had imposed, an atmosphere in which Punch was prone to bark, rail, and scream at his troops, brooking no questions or opposition.

Some found this atmosphere brought the best out of them. George Armstrong tuned out Imlach's tirades and left the dressing room determined to win for himself and his teammates. Some were irritated, like Bob Baun or Carl Brewer, who questioned Imlach's trading skills and even his sanity. Others were driven to depression, such as Frank Mahovlich. In extreme cases, it pushed them out of the fold altogether, toward other teams who prospered at the Leafs' expense.

Some of the young bucks Imlach inherited had been Marlboro stalwarts such as Bob Pulford, Billy Harris, Bob Nevin, Carl Brewer, and Bob "Boomer" Baun. Others were the fabled St. Michael's College Majors — guys like Tim Horton; Dick Duff; a slick-moving centre from Noranda, Quebec named Dave Keon; and Frank Mahovlich, a phenomenon from Northern Ontario. To supplant these up-and-comers, Imlach used his considerable skills as a hockey flesh peddler. He called upon his powers of persuasion to acquire castoffs from other crews who could bring his ship home.

One of his first coups was to secure career AHL goaltender Johnny Bower. He reckoned that at 33, the one-time Ranger had something left in the tank. Bower could still poke-check an opposing forward and take the other guy's feet out from under him until he slid on his belly into the corner boards. This move separated the forward from the puck and, most of the time, resulted in no penalty. The coming 2 years proved Punch right on the money when it came to Bower. "The China Wall" won one Vezina Trophy outright and shared another, both in a Leafs uniform.

Making a deal with the Rangers for a tall Ukrainian boy from Sudbury who had a big nose and a wild skating style didn't quicken any pulses right away, but Eddie Shack proved to be an entertaining forward who occasionally put the puck in the net.

Imlach, however, still had to score that one big deal to show the hockey world Toronto was serious about reasserting its place atop the hockey heap. It happened when Jack Adams effectively drove Red Kelly out of Detroit and moved him to New York without the player's consent. Kelly refused to report and retired, nullifying the swap. Punch saw his chance. He talked to the disenchanted star and sent Marc Rheaume to Motown for the rights to the Norris and three-time Lady Byng winner. He even acceded to Kelly's request that he get off the blue line and convert to centre. It was a move that paid off handsomely; Kelly notched his first 20-goal season the following year.

There were other trades down the road that ultimately caused the Leafs juggernaut to brake sharply. They were future-is-now deals, geared to producing short-term results, or made in a fit of Imlach pique. These deals threw sand in the wonderful machinery that showed so much promise at the dawn of the 1960s, the last great era for Leaf fans.

Conn Smythe recalled in his memoirs that Punch was the worst general manager he ever hired ... and the best coach. Call it feel, instinct, call it what you will, Imlach's skill in handling a game situation made the Major's mouth water. Back in the days of Hap Day, Smythe had instituted a system of sending a messenger boy down to the Leafs bench from his spot in the third-tier seats to tell the coach to send a certain

Punch Imlach

man out on the ice in a certain situation. To his delight, Conn found that Punch managed to get the man in question on long before the winded youth reached the bench. Only a few instances of Imlach's apparent clairvoyance were enough to impress Smythe to leave his charge alone during a game.

What that vote of confidence, Imlach, who had leap-frogged from the obscurity of Springfield to the heady atmosphere of Toronto within months, decided to have some fun with the situation. Perhaps to take the pressure off his men, he told all who would listen that the Leafs would make the playoffs, no question about it. The rest of the league laughed, for the two previous seasons were about as dismal an outing as an NHL team could have. Toronto registered only 54 points in 70 games in 1957–1958, only 57 the year before that.

Nor was the math on Imlach's side as season's end approached. With five games to go in the regular season, the fifth-place Leafs still trailed the Rangers by seven points. However, in one of the most incredible finishes of all time, Toronto won all five games to overtake the collapsing New Yorkers by a point to nail down the final playoff spot.

Punch had made believers of Leafs fans everywhere. He raised eyebrows and hopes higher in the first round of the playoffs when they toppled the heavily-favoured Bruins in seven games. They came back to earth in the finals against the mighty Canadiens, bowing to Montreal in five games. The following year, the Leafs didn't just scrape by. With a vengeance, they made the playoffs with 79 points. Then they polished off the Wings in six games, before falling again to Rocket and the Habs, this time in four straight. Fortunately for the Leafs, and the rest of the league, Maurice Richard retired after the playoffs. Montreal's incredible string of five consecutive Cups was soon to end.

By the spring of 1962, Stanley Cup fever hit Toronto hard, and no one wanted a vaccine. The veterans Imlach had called on — Bower, Kelly, Shack, Armstrong, Stanley and Olmstead — complemented the homegrowns — Keon, Mahovlich, Brewer, and Baun — to bring playoff glory to a town starved for it. First, they stifled Andy Bathgate and the Rangers in six games, before setting their sights on the defending Stanley Cup champion Black Hawks. With an effective mix of offensive spark and defensive hockey (generally consisting of wresting the puck away from the enemy attacker, clearing the zone, or simply icing the puck dozens of times), the Leafs fended off Chicago in six games to take the Cup, Toronto's first in 11 years!

However, it was also in that moment of euphoria that some of the worst traits of Punch Imlach began to emerge. Some players were sipping beers while changing into their civvies for the triumphal journey home from Chicago, when their coach stormed in, breathing fire, hollering that the team bus was leaving in 15 minutes, and anyone not on that bus wouldn't be on the team the next year. After the players stopped shaking their heads in disbelief, Eddie Shack joked that the 15-minute beer was invented!

The proud Imlach had his cup, and his ego was only growing. The following year did nothing to slow that ego down. The Leafs finished first in the league's regular season, with 82 points. They needed only two games more than the minimum to recapture the cup against Montreal and Detroit. More than that, rookie defenceman Kent Douglas was added to the list of recent Calder Trophy winners in Leaf uniform. Winning was becoming a habit in Hogtown, and Leaf fans everywhere lapped it up. They made Saturday nights almost holy, gathering round the tube starting at 9 p.m. to see how the Leafs would notch yet another win. Punch Imlach, by luck or by design, was a national celebrity, and he reveled in it.

Even as hockey success was becoming comfortable in English Canada's biggest city, critics say rot was setting in. Hockey historians note that Imlach received a letter from the father of a slender, dazzling, 12 year old defenceman who was playing rings around older opponents in his hometown of Parry Sound. The letter asked the Leafs general manager to come out to watch his son play. Amazingly, Imlach handed the letter to one of his subordinates to have chief scout Bob Davidson issue a reply, instead of answering it personally, heading out to Parry Sound, and seeing what all the fuss was about. The Boston Bruins, eager for a saviour, sent a scout who all but lived in Parry Sound that winter. The Bruins snapped up the hockey prodigy at once. This sense that everything was all right in Leafs Nation and this failure to follow through on improvements caused Bobby Orr to become a legend as a Bruin, even though the youngster's initial fervour was to wear blue and white.

Imlach was loyal to veteran goalies like Johnny Bower, and later, Terry Sawchuk, (acquired from Detroit). This loyalty blinded him to the merits of promoting young goalies whose rights the Leafs organization owned, such as Gerry Cheevers, or local net minders the Leafs never thought worth their time, such as Ken Dryden. In time, both Cheevers and

Dryden achieved stardom, Hall of Fame status, and yes, Stanley Cups, with other clubs, while Leafs fortunes continued to go downhill.

The success he'd enjoyed with veterans led him into swaps for other men, long in the tooth, but who supposedly could produce for him right away, at the expense of younger men around whom he could have built the team of the future. After all, he reasoned, he hadn't gone wrong in nearly six years in the Leafs' front office, and why should he change? His future-is-now approach to player deals continued.

One deal fraught with risk, however, sent Leafs stalwarts Bob Nevin, Dick Duff, and Rod Seiling to the Rangers late in the 1964 season, for Don McKenney and Andy Bathgate. Nevin and Seiling moved on to be productive Rangers for years to come, Duff three times a Cup winner in Montreal. Within a year, McKenney was placed on waivers, and Bathgate was dealt away to Detroit. Moreover, some of the Leafs veterans figured the deal tinkered with the chemistry of the club that had been so successful. (Baun would state for the record that the Leafs should have won 10 Stanley Cups in the 1960s, suggesting it would have happened if the trade hadn't broken what didn't need fixing.)

Still, if his magic as a horse trader showed signs of waning, Punch still had a very tight grip on the team that wore Toronto colours. With his coach's hat on, Punch told all who would listen that his club was in shape, ready, and determined to win it all. He drove his charges even harder.

He made them practise every day, even though some were getting older, slower, and wonkier.

It took the maximum 14 games, but the Leafs vanquished Montreal and Detroit once again and took the Cup home for the third straight time. The memory of that 1964 final series against the Wings causes Leafs fans of all ages to become dewy-eyed: Baun, hobbling on what would later be found to be a broken leg, intercepted a clearing pass from Al Langlois and slammed it home past Sawchuk in overtime to give the Leafs sudden life. This win forced game seven, in which Baun, Bower, and the boys shut-out Bower's longtime fishing partner, Gordie Howe, and the Motowners 4–0. The Gardens rafters shook once again with the deafening roar of crazed fans as the final bell sounded that humid Saturday night in April. The old warriors grouped around the tall silver mug, smiling and savouring the moment. They posed for one hard-earned, informal team picture, for this Cup win was special!

Two years of first round failure followed those Leafs triumphs. A third straight year of frustration appeared in the offing, especially starting in mid-January 1967, when the Leafs lost 10 straight, despite Imlach's best efforts to whip the team into shape with two-a-day workouts. One morning, Imlach collapsed from what doctors at first called "complete exhaustion." Suspicion grew that Punch had sustained a heart attack, for there were reports of pains shooting up his arm. Whatever the tale of the ticker, the club won six of their next seven, as King Clancy, the jolly Irishman, spelled Punch behind the bench. Players in Imlach's doghouse appeared to be flourishing under Clancy, and they were getting more opportunities to play.

Imlach, who sensed a mutiny by the players over his treatment of them, dispatched the affable Armstrong to defuse it with an airing-out session in January. Imlach was back on his feet in March, took the reins again, and posted a 6–5 record the rest of the regular schedule. The Leafs won a respectable 32 games and finished third.

Still, things were far from rosy. Imlach had always found Mahovlich a convenient target. He even deliberately mispronounced his name "Ma-HOLLO-vitch" — and he never took into account Frank's somewhat sensitive nature. Punch conveyed the idea that players were not greater than the team and that they could be easily discarded. He resisted special handling of anybody. Mahovlich was hospitalized that year with a stress-related illness, and despite a reputation as an explosive scorer, notched only 18 goals that year. The unease between fragile Frank and his "commanding officer" coach had teammates mystified.

Punch could never control Carl Brewer, a man who skated to the beat of his own drum. He was a bundle of nerves in the lead-up to the game (no doubt from the riding of his coach) but, inexplicably cool as a cucumber once the puck was dropped. One night, after a successful outing, Punch came back to Brewer's spot in the dressing room and congratulated him on what he thought was Brewer's best game ever. The defenceman, looking to get a reaction out of his mentor, shrugged it off and said it was like any other game, provoking a blue streak that sent Punch ranting and raving out of the room.

By the mid-60s, Brewer had had enough of Imlach. He returned to school to get his degree, obtained reinstatement as an amateur, and joined Canada's National Team program, before returning to the NHL in the latter part of the decade … with the Red Wings. In Detroit, he again showed flashes of his former brilliance, without courting the ulcer that always threatened under Imlach.

Bob Baun, nicknamed "Boomer" for his thunderous checks, also proved a thorn in Imlach's side, particularly when younger Leafs came to him for advice on contract negotiations before going into Punch's office. (Imlach always waited till training camp before signing players, operating on their insecurity over making the club.) A rare athlete of his time with some savvy for business, Baun could decipher the legalese of young players' contracts and arm them with some knowledge on how to deal with Punch. Eventually, the coach and general manager got wind of this, erupted at Baun and all who had ventured by his seat in the locker room. They gradually reduced Boomer's ice time so that by the 1967 play-offs, Baun was hardly playing at all.

Sick bay that 1967 season also included the goalies. Neither Bower nor Sawchuk, who'd collaborated years before on winning a Vezina Trophy, managed to play 30 games that season. This left room for understudies like veteran Bruce Gamble, rookie Al Smith, and Rochester call-up, Gary "Suitcase" Smith (no relation). Punch must have realized that position players, notably Armstrong, Horton, Kelly, Stanley, Pronovost were also long in the tooth and probably near the end of their careers. There would be no blockbuster deals at the trading deadline that year, so the team had to sink or swim with much the same line-up that been blown out in four straight by the Habs the previous spring.

This special group of men, whether anxious to go out with a bang to showcase themselves for upcoming NHL expansion or infused with the centennial spirit of 1967, looked deep within themselves for ways to win that Cup, against all odds.

Imlach returned to his old tyrannical ways and housed his team at the Rock Haven Motel in Peterborough, rather than letting his players go home and relax as the playoff round against Chicago loomed. The move was likely aimed at creating an army-unit mentality, but it almost backfired. The players fumed, and their disarray showed in a 5–2 opening night loss. Imlach adjusted in game two by having his boys adopt a strategy of bumping MVP Stan Mikita around. That, and the dreadful Chicago Stadium ice, combined for a 3–1 Leaf victory. That strategy of slowing the Chicago shooters down worked, as Toronto's "Over-the-Hill Gang" took the series in six games.

Throughout this series and the next one against

Montreal, Imlach directed his defencemen to take the face-offs in their own end. He reasoned that if they lost the draw, they could then lean on the opposing centre, tying up either stick, skates, or body, until a Leaf teammate gathered in the puck. Most often, for all the opposition might howl, the referee's arm stayed down.

Psychologically, Imlach had another ace up his sleeve. Toe Blake's defending Stanley Cup champions had come into the final series hot as the proverbial two-dollar pistol, riding a 15-game unbeaten streak, including a four-game whitewashing of the Rangers in the first round. The jockey of that streak was Rogatien Vachon, a 21 year old goalie who only a year before had flunked a tryout with the Junior Canadiens. Imlach saw his angle. He slammed Vachon as a "Junior B" goalie and added his team was ready to show Vachon was human.

In game one, Vachon rammed the words down Imlach's throat, as he seemed perfectly at ease stonewalling Toronto 6–2. It was the Leaf defence that seemed to need a lesson, as Tim Horton was on the ice for five goals, Allan Stanley for four.

Imlach held to his old strategy of tight checking — the Montreal forwards were practically wearing Leafs players around their necks. The tack seemed to take, as Toronto got under the skin of Montreal players. Stanley belted Henri Richard with his head down, which negated the "Pocket Rocket" for the rest of the series. Brian Conacher, son of the legendary Lionel, tussled with Claude Larose of the Habs and cut him for seven stitches. Bower and Sawchuk, for all their aches, pains and aging, held the Canadiens off while their mates took a 3–2 series lead.

Imlach still engaged in psychological war with Vachon. He upgraded the young goalie to "Junior A," but by then, Blake had replaced him for the next game with Gump Worsley.

Game six placed a special urgency on winning, for it was scheduled for Tuesday, May 2, 1967, and all four Leafs losses had taken place on Thursdays. Superstitious or not, denizens of Leafs Nation prayed for Punch's bunch to finish off Blake's team, rather than let them off the hook for game seven back in Montreal on Thursday.

Imlach kept his team intact, going with the troubled Sawchuk in goal. He continued to give Horton, Stanley, Pronovost and Hillman their regular turns on defence, however badly they may have been burned earlier in the series. He counted on the younger guys to lean on Montreal's forwards and maybe see their way clear to a scoring opportunity.

Goals from role players like Jim Pappin, another Imlach antagonist, and Ron Ellis, staked Toronto to a 2–0 lead. Dick Duff beat Sawchuk early in the third, and the blood pressure in the venerable Gardens again headed skyward. The final minute of the third period, on what was already a warm, spring night, was the stuff of legend.

Bob Pulford, who became a successful hockey executive himself, knew what Imlach had up his sleeve in that late hour. He was gathering his veterans for one last, fleeting wisp of glory. This was fully justified when Stanley and Kelly combined to win the draw from Beliveau, spirit the puck to Pulford, then over to Armstrong into a net emptied of the veteran Worsley.

Tragically, Pulford was right. NHL expansion, retirement, executive bungling, criminal activity in the front office, the onset of a players' union, and Punch's own intransigent ways all combined to gut the once proud Maple Leafs franchise, with no hope of rebuilding for years to come.

Even during the Cup years, there had always been tension between Imlach and club president, Stafford Smythe. In fact there had been tension as early as the 1950s, when Stafford had coveted the GM's role. In 1969, Smythe pulled the plug on his coach and general manager within hours of a humiliating playoff sweep by a Boston Bruin team led by the same Bobby Orr whom Imlach had so curtly ignored only eight years before.

However, George "Punch" Imlach pulled himself from the ashes and reinvented himself as general manager, coach, and public face of the expansion Buffalo Sabres starting in 1970. He stoked his team with stars like Gilbert Perreault, Richard Martin, Craig Ramsay, and Danny Gare. Collectively, these young Turks caught fire in 1975. They knocked over a Bowman-coached Montreal squad and catapulted Imlach into the Stanley Cup finals for the seventh time. Unfortunately, that squad ran into a Philadelphia team with guys named Clarke, Leach, McLeish, Schultz, Saleski, Dupont, and Parent — players who were just too strong for the neophytes from Buffalo.

By the end of the 1970s, Punch had been drummed out of Buffalo and was back in Toronto, but it wouldn't be the same. Imlach's dictatorial style was discredited as belonging to an earlier time when players feared for their jobs and did as they were told. The once and future boss of Maple Leaf Gardens locked horns with Darryl Sittler, Lanny McDonald, Tiger Williams, and Mike Palmateer and eventually dealt them away. Older holdouts from the 1960s came in, including Carl Brewer, creating locker room tension and destroying team harmony.

Morale in Leafs Nation remained low for another decade, due in large part to the interference of Harold Ballard. He was a man who had been convicted of fraud and whose ownership fostered an atmosphere in which mediocrity flourished, pedophiles practiced with impunity, and nothing positive emerged. Within two years, Imlach was again dumped as unceremoniously as the last time. When he returned to the Gardens from another bout of heart trouble, he found his parking spot had been reassigned.

Still, if his trading strategy stank of the quick-fix, if his treatment of players prevented long-term success by fostering bad blood, and if his ego rubbed players, peers, and reporters the wrong way, credit is due to Punch Imlach for the determination and single-mindedness he brought to his job, and the results it brought Toronto. Love him or hate him, Leafs fans will never again see his like — his arrogance, or the thrill of his success.

And, oh, what a thrill it was!

Chapter 7
Scotty Bowman: The Ultimate Winner

The air over the ice at the Joe Louis Arena was thick with doubt that Tuesday night, April 17, 2002. The heavily favoured Detroit Red Wings were in a death struggle with the Vancouver Canucks. It was game one of the Western Conference quarter final, the first entrance ramp on the long road to the Stanley Cup. The Wings had scorched the NHL during the regular season with 116 points. They had a line-up resembling a Hall of Fame induction ceremony — names like Shanahan, Hull, Larionov, Hasek, Robitaille, Chelios, and most of all, Yzerman. The Canucks were the West's eighth seed, and they were probably feeling lucky even to be in the post-season. Yet, there they were, playing the monsters of Michigan in their own backyard to a 3-all draw, late in regulation time.

Detroit's coach had seen enough. He called a time out and summoned his on-ice workhorses to the bench area. This was not a pep-talk, more a pause, think, and reflect session. Scotty Bowman gave his charges the silent treatment and left it up to them to find the way out of the corner into which they appeared to have painted themselves. After all, they'd won the President's Trophy and made millions of dollars doing it. Many of them had been through this situation before and even won Stanley Cups. They were experienced, grizzled veterans, who knew that the Canucks would come out loosey-goosey against a home side on which the pressure rested squarely. If they didn't know what to do by now, well … .

Normally, this is where the reader would be told the tactic worked, and that Detroit scored the overtime goal to begin the quest that would land the Wings their tenth Stanley Cup, and Bowman his ninth. The fact is that the Canucks won that game. They also won the next one in Detroit, before the ship was righted and the Wings took charge. However, such was an example of the mind games on which William Scott Bowman made his reputation, but which didn't always endear him to his players.

Another such game had been played two decades before, when a young Tom Barrasso had won the Vezina and Calder trophies as a rookie goaltender for Bowman's Buffalo Sabres, but somehow found himself off his game the following season. To hear reports from teammates, he "couldn't fit his head in the locker room." Bowman acted decisively and sharply. He sent the backstop down to Buffalo's farm team in Rochester. As expected, Barrasso didn't take the demotion well and threatened to "kick the shit out of somebody." In time, he reported, changed his attitude, and went on to win two Cups in Pittsburgh, one with his old mentor/nemesis, Bowman.

Some didn't take to Bowman's measures at all and made no bones about telling him so. One of Bowman's early challenges in Detroit was to keep the volatile Bob Probert in line. Bowman not only kept Probert out of fights, but away from his self-destructive tendencies toward drink and drugs. One night when Probert was stepping out for his shift, Bowman cautioned him yet again about mixing it up.

Probert glared back at the legend behind the bench and growled, "There's just one guy I want to [fight] with right now, and I'm lookin' at him."

Probert was not much longer for the Motor City, where he'd made his name as a gladiator on the ice and a troublemaker off it.

Another Red Wing, Shawn Burr, called Bowman "the most disrespectful person I've ever met. He's just a mean man with no social skills."

Still another, Dino Ciccarelli said, "As a coach, he's the best ever. But as a person, he's a jerk. Ask anyone who has ever played for him and they'll tell you the same thing."

However, his defenders say, well, too bad; he was a

winner. Brendan Shanahan was in that camp. "People say they hate Scotty Bowman. So what?"

Anyone who argues that a domineering coach couldn't survive in the current NHL climate of player agents and six-figure salaries would clearly have met his match in Scotty Bowman. He was an exception in other ways, too. He was a man who carved out a dazzling coaching career without turning pro as a player. In 27 years as an NHL coach, he never experienced a losing season. Bowman made his name in junior coaching ranks and then grabbed the reins of an NHL expansion team before he made his way to hockey's capital, Montreal. There, he ensured a string of successes of which his mentor, Toe Blake, would be proud. Then he inherited the torch from a fallen colleague in Pittsburgh and brought them to the summit, before restoring Detroit's status as Hockeytown once more.

Poker players like to describe better players by saying, "When I have the cards, I clean the table. When they have the cards, they clean the room." For sure, Bowman cleaned the room in Montreal and Detroit. He knew how to handle the big names on his bench, and he knew how to make sure there was room for everyone else. Many times, a team's line-up is stocked with major stars, with major reputations, attitudes, and salaries, and they are expected to win right away and don't. Scotty Bowman knew how to get the most out of every player, regardless of his talents, to help the team win. Through his aloof ways, he kept even the brightest stars on edge, demanding more of them all the time. Many of the great names in the game — Guy Lafleur, Ken Dryden, Bob Gainey, Steve Shutt, Mario Lemieux, Steve Yzerman, and Brett Hull — admit they became better under the watchful eye of Scotty Bowman.

William Scott Bowman was born in the Montreal-area town of Verdun in September 1933. By his late teens, he had already made his name as a fine checking winger with the Montreal Junior Canadiens. However, in a playoff game when he was 18, Bowman took a high-stick from Jean-Guy Talbot of the Trois-Rivières Club and sustained a five-inch gash to his scalp that needed 14 stitches to close. Reports circulated that Bowman had sustained a skull fracture that required a steel plate, effectively knocking him out of the game for life, but these stories were untrue. Bowman missed one game and tried to come back to aid the Junior Habs in their playoffs, but he suffered from headaches and blurred vision. He was never the same player.

Scotty Bowman discovered, as do many ex-players, how coaching can provide a career extension. He just did so sooner than most. He first coached in minor hockey ranks in Montreal while working at a paint store during the day. On lunch breaks, he would sneak into the Forum to watch the NHL Canadiens practise. He took up coaching assignments in Junior B ranks, before being hired to coach the Junior Canadiens in time for their move to Ottawa-Hull. In each of his first two years, Bowman's juniors made it to the Memorial

Cup final. The team won the Cup on his second try in 1958. His team's general manager was Sam Pollock, later to become Montreal's "Godfather"; his captain was Ralph Backstrom, a mainstay of the Canadiens' Stanley Cup teams of the mid to late 1960s.

A move to Peterborough led to another Memorial Cup final in 1961. Scotty took on a variety of junior coaching and minor league scouting jobs with the Canadiens' organization throughout the 1960s.

People who lived through the turbulent 1960s cite shifting social and sexual mores. They remember more frequent questioning of authority and discussions about citizens' rights as a society and what to do to preserve them. This wind of change engulfed the hockey world as well, with the emergence of a players' union, the expansion of the NHL from six teams to 12, and the recognition of hockey as a truly international game. More exposure, more fans, and more money were out there to be had from playing the game of hockey, and Scotty Bowman was among its chief beneficiaries.

Expansion brought hockey to six centres in the good old USA. Some of them had long-stretching minor league hockey traditions like Pittsburgh, Minnesota, St. Louis, and Philadelphia. Some franchises were granted more for their marquee value like Los Angeles and Oakland. Scotty had the good fortune of starting his NHL coaching career as an assistant in St. Louis. His connections with former Bruin general manager Lynn Patrick paid off, as Bowman had coached

Lynn's son Craig as a junior. It was agreed that Patrick would coach the forwards, and Bowman would change the defensive players on the bench.

Just a few weeks into the 1967–1968 season, Lynn pulled a fast one on the 34 year old Bowman and handed him the head coaching baton, confident Bowman could handle the veteran-laden Blues. At first glance, winning the players over seemed a tall order, with defencemen like Barclay and Bob Plager, Doug Harvey, Noel Picard, Jean-Guy Talbot (he of the high stick that ended Bowman's playing career), and Al Arbour; forwards like Ron Stewart, Dickie Moore, and Larry Keenan, backstopped by Mr. Goalie himself, Glenn Hall. Many of them were older than Bowman was; however, Bowman had known many of these men, having coached them or against them in junior. He eventually settled in.

"I never did anything foolish with them, but I wasn't intimidated by them, either," he told commentator Dick Irvin.

Expansion added another round of playoffs, making the task of winning the Cup even more exhausting than before, but the Blues were survivors. They knocked off the Philadelphia Flyers and Minnesota North Stars — in seven games each — before introducing the Missouri city to the heady atmosphere of a Stanley Cup final against the legendary Canadiens and the equally legendary coach Blake. Victories were excruciatingly elusive; the Blues lost in four straight, each by one goal, but Bowman's long in the tooth bunch had put hockey on the map at the mouth of the Mississippi!

With help from Jacques Plante, Bowman's Blues were in the finals the next two years after that. Again, they were swept into dustbins, by the Habs in 1969 and then by a Boston Bruin team with all the looks of an approaching dynasty — Esposito, Hodge, McKenzie, Sanderson, and most of all, a swashbuckling defenceman named Orr. It was the last time ever that St. Louis was that deep into the playoffs, and much of it was Scotty Bowman's doing. It may have spoiled the Salomon family, the St. Louis owners, who appeared to expect that playoff revenue stream cascading into early May every year. Whether it was due to that expectation or just time for a change, Scotty Bowman was cut loose by the Blues in the spring of 1971. Events within and without hockey ensured that he would be not left staring at his pink slip for long.

In the fall of 1970, tensions between Canada's two founding peoples boiled over in Quebec, during what was called The October Crisis. It began with the abduction of a British embassy official by one wing of the terrorist Front de Libération du Québec, and the kidnapping and eventual assassination of a provincial cabinet minister by another. The federal government of Pierre Trudeau responded by invoking *The War Measures Act*, curtailing civil rights and imprisoning individuals without trial. The tensions took years to subside, resulting in attempts to preserve French within Quebec by passing discriminatory language laws and giving muscle to a separatist movement. Much as the youth of the world had adopted a mindset of not trusting anyone over 30, so were those of Quebec of a mind not to trust anyone who did not know how to speak French.

By the spring of 1971, the tensions appeared to be overtaking the Canadiens' dressing room as the club took the ice for an improbable Stanley Cup final series against the Black Hawks in Chicago. This was a rebuilding year for Montreal, the 1970 squad having missed the playoffs for the first time since time began, or so it seemed. The all too real world of Quebec politics appeared to filter into the picture. Having been denied a regular shift in game five, Henri Richard came out with a verbal swipe at caretaker coach, Al MacNeil, calling him the worst coach he'd ever played for. While all the attention on Richard seemed to unite the rest of the team in common cause and carry them to victories in games six and seven — and yet another Stanley Cup — the damage from the Pocket Rocket's remark had been done. MacNeil was out the door, and a new coach, preferably fluent in French and English, was sought out. William Scott Bowman, long time Hab organization man and Stanley Cup finalist three times over, seemed tailor-made for the situation.

It was a heady time for the 37 year old Bowman to arrive back home in Montreal, in part because of his reunion with old manager, Sam Pollock, from the junior coaching days, and in part because the Canadiens were already the gold standard for hockey. He knew that a winning tradition dating back to 1916 raised expectations to just where he wanted them.

"I knew that when the playoffs came," Bowman told

Irvin, "the team was going to give the ultimate performance. You expected it and I think it spurred them on."

For players like Frank Mahovlich, who had laboured under the cantankerous and unrelenting Punch Imlach, Scotty Bowman was a breath of fresh air. "He ran a fairly good practice," the "Big M" said, adding that Bowman didn't push energy out of players in those practices that could be better used in a game.

"There were a lot of games that I left in practice in Toronto. When I got to Montreal, I felt like a tiger out there, that I still had something left." Mahovlich was among those who helped hoist Bowman's first Stanley Cup in 1973. But it was just a taste of things to come.

Pollock had already done his incoming coach a favour weeks before, having made a deal with Oakland for their first-round draft pick. The Seals had finished dead last in the NHL standings, and this gave Montreal the first pick overall. They used that pick to draft a saviour out of the Quebec Junior League, a goal-scoring genius who had led the Quebec Remparts to the Canadian junior championship, destined to be a luminary in Montreal as bright as Morenz, the Rocket, and Beliveau.

Bowman's challenge was to break young Guy Lafleur into the ranks gradually and not burn him out too soon. For the first two years, Bowman spotted his new charge here and there, holding off on granting him a regular shift. Guy responded with 29 goals his first year, 28 his second, and 21 his third. These weren't bad numbers for a young player, but hardly superstar stats, either. In 1975–1976, all that changed, as Guy played more regularly and put Montreal on its last great Stanley Cup binge!

Before that, signs of the Bowman legend were making themselves visible.

In March of 1972, toward the end of his first season in Montreal, Bowman almost died in a St. Louis hotel fire. Several players commandeered a ladder to get their new coach out of his room. When they succeeded and he finally came to, the first thing he did was count the players for curfew (no joke!).

"I'll tell you something," he said to his biographer, Douglas Hunter. "It takes an incident like that to really unite a bunch of guys together as a unit." While not recommended, the fire rescue proved a great team-building exercise.

No question all of the Canadien players were on the same page in 1975–1976, in a way few teams had been before or since. They finished the regular season with 127 points, losing only 11 of 76 games. Lafleur became the scorer everyone knew he would be, with his second straight 50-goal season, registering 125 points. The team enjoyed a first-round bye. Then they waltzed through to the finals with a sweep over Chicago and a five-game drubbing of the Islanders, before meeting the Broad Street Bullies from Philadelphia.

It was there that Bowman's talent for match ups showed itself, as he used three different centres against the Flyers' big line of Bobby Clarke, Bill Barber, and Reggie Leach. Bowman sent Jacques Lemaire, Doug Risebrough, and Doug Jarvis out to keep that line offbalance and rob it of its scoring menace. The magic worked; the Habs turned Philly aside in four straight, and while Leach of the Flyers took the Conn Smythe Trophy. Lord Stanley was back in Montreal, this time for an extended stay.

1977 proved the year before was no fluke, with "The Flower" in full bloom winning the Hart Trophy, Steve Shutt firing 60 goals to set a record for left wingers, Ken Dryden and Bunny Larocque combining for the Vezina Trophy, and Larry Robinson taking the Norris Trophy as top blue liner. The team was the thing, and the Habs trampled over the regular season for 60 wins and 132 points. That time, the victims in the final were from Boston, the legend of Don Cherry's Lunchpail A.C. (referring to their blue-collar hard-working approach to hockey) having not yet come to life. Montreal triumphed over the Bruins in four straight, with Lemaire's overtime winner in game four sealing the deal.

Still, Bowman found, as had Blake, the challenge to keeping great teams great for a long period was in making great players feel "responsible." That meant the game wasn't going to take shape if those players didn't make it happen. At the same time, Bowman's philosophy was not to get too close to any one of the boys or make a player feel like his friend. Bowman's appreciation and respect for his stars was genuine, but he strove not to show it.

"[You couldn't be] saying things you maybe don't mean or couldn't back up," he told commentator Dick Irvin. "I just think it worked better for me that they knew I wasn't going to stroke them and I demanded they had to play well. Most of the time I think it worked."

It led to a reputation for abruptness and aloofness, as if their coach was going out of his way to make his players dislike him. Bowman was notorious for going to the papers to air his gripes about this player or that, especially around contract time, working on that unfortunate player's insecurities and anxieties. Once the sting of that treatment wore off, players were able to channel their efforts into winning.

Occasionally, he went too far. One day Bowman railed about Serge Savard's off-ice behaviour before the veteran defenceman got to the rink. Fortunately, Henri Richard informed the coach that telling Serge privately would have been the better remedy. Another time, Yvan Cournoyer voiced the team's objection to being drilled in morning practice as punishment after a loss, and Bowman stopped employing it.

However, Peter Mahovlich, Frank's younger brother, complained to reporters about his lack of ice time under Bowman, having been moved off the Lafleur line. He soon found himself shipped to Pittsburgh. Whining to the press about ice time crossed the line with Scotty Bowman.

While lots of coaches tossed around the idea of a system, Bowman purported not to have one. Henri Richard claimed the only system Bowman imposed on him was to get the puck out of the defensive zone as fast as he could. But Bowman always had a game plan. For him, coaching boiled down to three things: preparation, practice, and motivation. While he felt line match ups were overrated, being able to change on the fly effectively was paramount, and coaches around the league agreed that no one was better at that delicate art than Scotty Bowman, such was his degree of preparedness.

Another skill Bowman had was to know the role of each player. He also learned how to brook resistance from some players, if it was inevitable. He reckoned that production from a snarky winger made that guy's attitude a bit easier to take.

"I don't think you can let a star player run a team," Scotty said, "but you can take a little more aggravation from him if he's going to perform according to his ability."

A coach did what it took to win. Scotty Bowman knew that, and the record showed it.

In 1978, Cherry's boys from Boston almost did the unthinkable. They pushed the Canadiens to the wall in the Stanley Cup final and knotted the series at two games apiece, after a memorable game four slugfest between Bruin spark plug, Stan Jonathan, and a beanpole defenceman Bowman had sent out, Gilles Lupien. Bowman ended up with egg on his face and Lupien with lumps, as the shorter Jonathan made mincemeat of the towering Lupien before a raucous Boston crowd. The Habs would not be denied, however. They took the next two games by identical 4–1 scores. Robinson, with 17 helpers, skated off with the Smythe, Les Glorieux with the Cup.

Bowman suspected that 1979 would be his final go-round with the Canadiens in strictly a coaching role. He had coveted a managerial post in Montreal or elsewhere, and he knew that Sam Pollock, his old mentor, would soon be stepping down as Habs' GM. He kept his eye off politics and on winning another Cup with a bunch of players who were on the way out as well. The result was a Cup run unlike any other.

The Stanley Cup semifinal pitted Montreal against bitter rival Boston once again. Lafleur later acknowledged that, harsh as he sometimes was on his players, Bowman never got out-coached. Don Cherry proved Lafleur right. He committed the cardinal sin of sending one too many Bruins over the boards in the third period of game seven, with his club up by a goal. Lafleur, as Bowman had trusted him to do so many times, took the game into his own hands, and he blasted the equalizer past a startled Gilles Gilbert to send the game into overtime. More heartache for the Beantowners came in the extra frame, when Yvon Lambert tallied to send Montreal through to the final against the surprising New York Rangers.

The Habs dropped game one against Fred Shero's Broadway Blueshirts, before Bowman got his troops refocused. They beat the Rangers in the next four, mostly on Gainey's heroics, and Bowman had his fifth Stanley Cup in Montreal, his fourth straight.

Days later, Dryden handed in his notice, followed by Lemaire, Cournoyer ... and Scotty Bowman, who announced he was leaving the town of his birth and scene of his greatest triumphs, to take up the twin posts of general manager and head coach in Buffalo. A new challenge awaited him.

Still, while there was much promise in the Queen City, with some good teams composed of great players, Bowman's tenure in Buffalo was full of individual regular-season glory (it was in Buffalo that he became the all-time winningest NHL coach, surpassing Dick Irvin), but numerous disappointments come playoff time. There wouldn't even be a finals appearance during Scotty's tenure on the Niagara Frontier. His teams consisted of the temperamental Tom Barrasso in goal, Gilbert Perreault, Richard Martin, Dave Andreychuk, and Mike Foligno on his forward lines, and defencemen Jim Schoenfeld and Phil Housley. His one regret, as he told an interviewer, was that even as he was absorbing the GM's job, he ended up returning to coaching with the Sabres several times. He found that sometimes wearing the two hats didn't work. Bowman left Buffalo in 1987 to take up broadcasting, before landing in Pittsburgh in the late 1980s as director of player development, alongside his old chum Craig Patrick, the general manager.

Bowman reveled in his new role, mostly a scouting one, until Penguin coach Bob Johnson fell ill with cancer in the summer of 1991. In something of a caretaker role, Bowman returned to the bench and molded the multi-talented Pittsburgh club into a well-rounded squad that could control play at both ends of the ice. This time, his charges were guys like Larry Murphy back on the blue line, his old Sabres antagonist, Barrasso, between the pipes, Rick Tocchet,

Ron Francis, Joe Mullen, Brian Trottier, and Jaromir Jagr up-ice. Oh, yes, there was also a tall, smooth-skating centreman claiming Gretzky's throne — Mario Lemieux.

In order to help the man with the number 66 on his Penguin jersey, Bowman took advantage of a change in the commercial schedule during network hockey telecasts. Bowman learned that the change involved four breaks a period of 60 seconds each, rather than the old seven breaks of 30 seconds each. By taking Lemieux off just before the 4, 8, 12, and 16 minute marks of every period and putting him right back on when the commercial was over, he was, in effect, double-shifting his captain, and Mario Lemieux was the type of player who needed a lot of ice time to be effective.

And, brother, was Mario effective! He led the Penguins to their second straight Cup with a sweep over the Chicago Blackhawks (the team's nickname had been combined to form one word in 1986). Bowman had his sixth Cup, and arguably, his most emotional, with a team still in mourning from the loss of their previous coach (Johnson had died the previous November). It was, as "Badger Bob" Johnson would have said, "a great day for hockey."

By the time Scotty Bowman left for Detroit in 1993, fans in the car capital had not seen so much as an appearance in the finals since 1966 and no Cups since 1955. This was all the more baffling, considering the talent on deck. There was Steve Yzerman, an elegant centre; Brendan Shanahan, a bruising forward with a scoring touch; Sergei Fedorov, a lethal sniper;

Kris Draper and Niklas Lidstrom back on defence, and Chris Osgood in goal. It took three years and two frustrating playoff series before Bowman returned the Cup to the Motor City, finishing off Eric Lindros and the Philadelphia Flyers in four straight games. He repeated the trick the next year against an upstart Washington Capitals squad.

One Stanley Cup run in 1997 featured a bitter semifinal series against Colorado, which included a full-scale brawl in the clinching game at the Joe Louis Arena. The Avalanche had eliminated Detroit the year before, after Claude Lemieux's head rear-ended Draper as the latter was leaving the ice. The cheap shot left a bad taste in many Red Wing mouths, and Bowman made sure his team came in with their dukes up. This included goaltender Mike Vernon, who battled his counterpart, Patrick Roy, in a mid-ice tussle, much to the delight of Bowman on the bench.

Yzerman had been merely a great player on weak teams in the pre-Bowman years, making dazzling offensive moves and scoring beautiful goals. Under Bowman's tutelage, the man they called "Detroit's Other Stevie Wonder" blossomed into a Hall of Famer by learning his way around his own end of the rink. In so doing, Yzerman became the embodiment of leadership. He was just the man to take the Wings to the next level.

According to former Sabre Craig Ramsay, Scotty "wouldn't put up with a purely checking guy who had no offensive skills," or a scorer who couldn't check. "He wants a guy who can legitimately play at both ends of the rink." A player will enjoy playing for a coach who lets him carry the puck, shoot, and score; he will be less willing to add checking to his list of job skills if it's not already there. Accordingly, Bowman pushed and pushed until he had brought out the best in Yzerman.

Bowman may have risked going too far in pressing to make Fedorov, a proven offensive talent, into a defenceman one year. Fedorov had won the Hart Trophy (Most Valuable Player), and the Frank Selke Trophy as best defensive forward. The experiment didn't take; Sergei grumbled over having to learn a new position too close to the playoffs one year.

"It's like having my hands tied behind a chair," he said.

Scotty moved Fedorov back to his post on the wing once the post-season got underway.

A three-year Stanley Cup lull was followed by a dream season in Detroit in 2001–2002, with a line-up that would make any coach salivate. Veterans such as Brett Hull, Dominik Hasek, Chris Chelios, and Luc Robitaille supplanted the men who had brought the Wings the hardware in previous years. In an imitation of the great Montreal teams of the 1970s, the Motowners ran up an impressive record of 51 wins and 116 points.

After finally getting traction against Vancouver, the Wings came roaring back to win four straight. Then they stopped St. Louis in five games, turning back their hated rivals from Colorado in seven games. That set up a final series with a hungry Carolina Hurricane contingent. After taking game one at the Joe Louis Arena in overtime, the 'Canes proved no match for an inspired Detroit squad, who knew it was the end of the line for some of them.

Scotty Bowman had served notice with Red Wing management that the ranks of the departing included him. He relished the moment, even putting his skates on to glide around the rink with the Cup one last time. It was his ninth championship, eclipsing the record of his old mentor, Toe Blake. He also had more wins than any other coach, 1,244, and he was leaving the game on top, as all coaches would like to.

He admitted to commentator Irvin that, with the years, coaching was getting harder for him. "I'm not as comfortable as I used to be in the hour leading up to a game. There are nights when you feel things are going well, and there are other nights when the game can't end soon enough. But when the game starts, it's a special time."

Scotty Bowman's devotion to hockey and his ability to make men rise to their full potential made his 27 years of coaching a special time for players, fans, and the game itself.

Perhaps Ken Dryden, hockey player, commentator and executive, Cornell grad, "Nader Raider," lawyer, and eventually federal cabinet minister, summed it up best: "Abrupt, straightforward, without flair or charm, [Bowman] seems cold and abrasive, sometimes obnoxious, controversial, but never colourful. He is complex, confusing, misunderstood, unclear in every way but one. He is a brilliant coach, the best of his time."

"I like him."

References

Barber, Jim. *Toronto Maple Leafs: Stories of Canada's Legendary Team*. Altitude Publishing. 2004.

Beliveau, Jean, Goyens, Chris & Allen Turowetz. *My Life in Hockey*. McClelland & Stewart, 1994

Cox, Damien & Stellick, Gord. *'67: The Maple Leafs, Their Sensational Victory, and the End of an Empire*. John Wiley & Sons. 2004.

Cruise, David & Griffiths, Alison. *Net Worth: Exploding the Myths of Pro Hockey*. Penguin Books 1991.

Dryden, Ken & McGregor, Roy. *Home Game: Hockey and Life in Canada*. McClelland & Stewart. 1989.

Fischler, Stan and Shirley. *Great Book of Hockey: More than 100 Years of Fire on Ice*. Publications International, 1997

Howe, Colleen and Gordie & Wilkins, Charles. *After the Applause*. McClelland & Stewart. 1989.

Hunter, Douglas. *Scotty Bowman: A Life in Hockey*. Penguin Group, 1998

Irvin, Dick. *Now Back to you, Dick: Two Lifetimes in Hockey*. McClelland & Stewart. 1988.

Irvin, Dick. *Behind the Bench*. McClelland & Stewart. 1993.

Leonetti, Mike. *Maple Leaf Legends: 75 Years of Toronto's Hockey Heroes*. Raincoast Books. 2002.

McFarlane, Brian. *Best of the Original Six*. Fenn Publishing. 2004.

Roxborough, Henry Hall. *The Stanley Cup Story*. Ryerson Press. 1966.

Smythe, Conn with Young, Scott. *If You Can't Beat 'em In the Alley*. McClelland & Stewart. 1981.

Photo Credits

Cover: AP Photo; Graphic Artists/Hockey Hall of Fame: page 107; Hockey Hall of Fame: page 19; Imperial Oil–Turofsky/ Hockey Hall of Fame: pages 36, 76, 90.

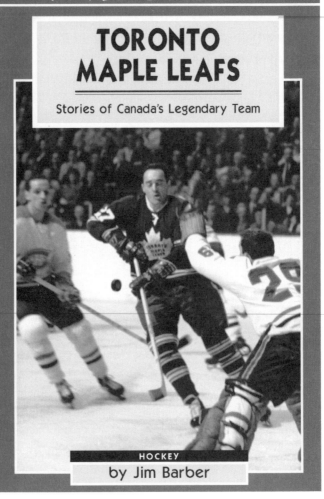

TRUE CANADIAN
AMAZING STORIES®

TORONTO MAPLE LEAFS

Stories of Canada's Legendary Team

HOCKEY

by Jim Barber

TORONTO MAPLE LEAFS
Stories of Canada's Legendary Team

"Since its construction in 1931, the Maple Leaf Gardens had seen its share of powerful, memorable moments and held its share of championship glory. But there was something different about this evening of May 2, 1967."

The Toronto Maple Leafs is one of Canada's greatest hockey franchises. From their humble beginnings in the 1920s, to their remarkable Stanley Cup victories of the 1940s and 1960s, to their team-building challenges of the 1990s and beyond, the Leafs have a history packed with exhilarating accomplishments and devastating setbacks. This is their story — the incredible story of a beloved Canadian institution.

 True stories. Truly Canadian.

ISBN 1-55153-788-5

OTHER AMAZING STORIES

These titles are available wherever you buy books. If you have trouble finding the book you want, call the Altitude order desk at **1-800-957-6888**, e-mail your request to: **orderdesk@altitudepublishing.com** or visit our Web site **at www.amazingstories.ca**

New AMAZING STORIES titles are published every month.